Warman's®

Bean Plush

FIELD GUIDE

2nd Edition

edited by Dan Brownell

Values and Identification

Published by

700 East State Street • Iola, WI 54990-0001
715-445-2214 • 888-457-2873
www.krausebooks.com

Our toll-free number to place an order or obtain a free catalog is (800) 258-0929.

Library of Congress Control Number: 2008924245

ISBN 13-digit: 978-0-89689-682-6

ISBN 10-digit: 0-89689-682-X

Designed by Kay Sanders

Edited by Dan Brownell

Printed in China

Dedication

To Julie Stephani, who made this book possible with her diligent research. Not only did she track down obscure information and ferret out current prices, she provided most of the photos from her personal collection. In fact, she bravely risked a Beanie Baby avalanche to get them. (Just ask her husband Bill.) Thank you Julie! May you someday have every collector's dream—a showcase big enough to display all your treasures.

Contents

Acknowledgments

I would like to extend a special thanks to the following people for their help in making this book possible:

Julie Stephani
Joan Gould
Bob Best
Kris Kandler
Sarah Werbelow
Cheryl Kell
Donna Mae Gerds
Toya Lund
Robyn Bjerke
Carrie Unze

Note on Prices: *This book is only a guide to values. Actual sale prices can vary due to many factors. Thus, the author and publisher are not responsible for the outcome of any transactions as a result of consulting this book.*

Introduction

Bean Plush Enthusiasts Become Collectors

A large number of enthusiasts became bean plush collectors in 1996 when the Ty Beanie Babies frenzy began. The soft plush animals were first manufactured in 1993, but it was the retirement of some Beanie Babies that took the market by storm. As quantities became limited, their value increased and collectors were quick to buy each one as it appeared in the stores—often in multiple quantities. H. Ty Warner began the ingenious marketing strategy with Beanie Babies, and other companies followed suit. Today, numerous collections are popular, including Shining Stars® and Webkinz®.

History

Ty® Bean Plush Toys

In 1993, H. Ty Warner released the "original nine" Beanie Babies, but it was several years before they became popular with collectors. Ty Inc. has now produced millions of the stuffed toys, and its success story is widely recognized in the business world as well as by collectors.

While plush toys had been around for years, Ty discovered the secret to marketing them, limiting the number of each item he produced and retiring them so their availability was limited. Ty targeted the child consumer and designed the Beanies small enough to fit in a pocket and priced so children could buy them with their allowance money. Another factor in Ty's success was the interactive Web site launched in 1996 that kept collectors informed regarding new Beanies and retirements, which stimulated sales. Ty limited its distributors to small gift stores, refusing to sell to large chain stores—and it is remarkable that Ty never advertised! The frenzy was created by word of mouth.

Ty limited the production of its first Beanies, but in response to public outcry has increased the number of most designs produced. This means highly sought-after Beanies are available to more people, but their greater availability also decreases their value on the secondary market.

More Excitement

A secondary Beanie frenzy began in 1997 when Ty partnered with McDonald's in a national campaign. Customers received a Teenie Beanie Baby with each Happy Meal. They were so popular that McDonald's stores ran out of them almost immediately, creating skyrocketing prices on the secondary market.

In late 1999, Ty announced it would retire all Beanie Babies, reigniting interest among collectors. However, after conducting a massive Internet survey, they decided to continue producing new Beanie Babies. Special cartoon characters were added, such as Garfield, SpongeBob, Blues Clues, Boblins, and Dora. A collection of NASCAR bears and Beatrix Potter characters are also new additions. Ty now has 22 lines of Beanies with the launching of Beanie Babies 2.0 in 2008 and continues as the leader in the plush toy market.

Collectors Remain Steadfast

Although the first wild frenzy has passed, numerous collectors are still actively pursuing their hobby today. Many are dedicated collectors who love accumulating the cushy little toys and continue buying, trading, and staying in touch with each other through a variety of Web sites. Those who have persevered have done so largely because they enjoy what they do, but they also have benefited financially from the shrinking number of collectors. When previous collectors no longer keep their collections in mint condition, the value of the remaining bean plush toys grows over time. Some rare ones fetch hundreds or even thousands of dollars.

As more common but well-preserved bean plush toys become increasingly rare, their value could rise significantly, too. The shrinking market provides another benefit to those who remain—enthusiasts can complete their collections by buying from those leaving the hobby.

Bean Plush Values

Whether you are buying or selling bean plush toys, it is important to know how much they are worth. We have researched the market to produce this handy pocket-sized reference you can easily take with you when searching for them. It is also a great reference to use to estimate the value of each one already in your collection. Add your personal notes to this book as the market prices fluctuate.

Several Markets Determine Prices

The prices in this guide are listed in U.S. dollars and are based on bean plush toys in mint condition. The values were determined by researching electronic and printed price guides as well as several online auction sites. They were current at the time of publication, but pricing is subjective and can change significantly over time. Krause Publications cannot be responsible for the outcome of any sales. The prices are a general guide, not a prediction of the results of any particular transaction. After all, price guides reflect average prices of many sales, while individual prices can vary greatly because they are affected by a number of factors—location, season, buyer demand, competition among sellers, and whether the seller is an individual or a business.

Individuals who sell at rummages sales or on Internet auctions often charge far lower prices than manufacturers and retailers. Hobbyists usually have very little overhead expense and just want to make a quick, one-time sale, whereas businesses have to pay ongoing overhead costs and must make substantial profit to survive. Although buyers may find much lower prices on Internet auctions, they take greater risks on the quality and authenticity of the products.

Determining Average Prices

Calculating average prices among retail and individual sellers is difficult, but each must be taken into account to accurately reflect prices. Buyers purchase from both sources, so neither can be disregarded. Often the result is that the average is a figure between two extremes. The prices in this book are weighted in favor of Internet auctions rather than retail stores because individuals can buy through both retail stores and auction sites, but they typically can sell only through auction sites. Because Internet auction sites provide greater accessibility to individual collectors, their prices create a more accurate measure of value.

Regardless of how sellers market their bean plush toys, the bottom line is that any item is only worth what someone is willing to pay for it at a particular time. That's the basic principle that drives a free-market economy.

Patience is a Virtue

In the bean plush toy market, as in any market, the key to success and satisfaction is patience. If you are still building your collection, consider your purchases a long-term investment. If you want to sell, don't rush. Timing is important. Demand can fluctuate widely even over a short period of time, greatly affecting the price. A particular bean plush toy that has been getting low prices may suddenly jump in value or vice-versa. Sometimes it is better to sell in sets. A set can be worth more when sold as a unit than when individual items are sold separately.

Authentication

Beware of Counterfeits

Whenever a highly profitable product reaches the market, you can be sure of two things. First, counterfeits will begin appearing soon after; and second, the quality of the counterfeits will continue to improve as long as the product is popular. The quality of fakes is certain to improve because counterfeiters are forced to keep one step ahead of increasingly savvy manufacturers, retailers, consumers, and other counterfeiters. Counterfeiters have a great deal at stake. Those who produce inferior reproductions are less likely to sell their goods and are more likely to be caught. Successful counterfeiters produce copies that can challenge even the experts, so consumers should take precautions to prevent being cheated.

Tips for Recognizing Fakes

1. Watch for online auctions in which sellers appear to be hiding something. A seller may be vague in the description or avoid giving clear answers to questions.

Of course, always be sure to check the seller's previous feedback to evaluate the person's reliability. Be especially careful when buying from a new seller. A seller who has not yet accumulated many feedback comments could be a risk. While the person may be honest but inexperienced, the lack of a significant sales record makes it difficult to determine the seller's credibility.

2. Be familiar with the characteristics of the manufacturer's swing tags to find noticeable errors or defects. For example, the tags may be cut or punched crooked or have borders that are uneven. The tags may also have misspelled words, poor grammar, strong colors, different font sizes, or ink that rubs off.

3. Look for poorly made plush toys, which may be made in the wrong shade or size, or have distorted or missing features. For example, the whiskers might be too long or short, in the wrong place, or the wrong color. In addition, the stitching could be uneven or sloppy, or the toy could be understuffed or overstuffed compared to the genuine article.

Ask An Expert

If you want to buy or sell an expensive bean plush toy, consider having it authenticated by an expert with an escrow service. Authentication will help keep a buyer from being cheated and will usually bring the seller a higher price—sometimes as much as 100 percent higher.

After the buyer and seller make a deal, the authenticator acts as an intermediary, accepting payment from the buyer and the bean plush toy from the seller. Once the toy has been verified as genuine, the authenticator sends it to the buyer and payment to the seller. The authenticator typically charges $10 to $12 for evaluating each plush toy plus $5 to $6 for shipping, for a total of $15 to $18 per item. Because normally it is the buyer who requests the service, the buyer usually bears the expense, although sometimes the buyer and seller split the cost. While this is a significant investment, it may well be worth it for a valuable plush toy. Be aware, however, that authenticators give expert opinions, not guarantees. If you choose to use an authenticator, be sure to hire one with a good reputation and verifiable credentials.

Care of Bean Plush Toys

To maintain the value of your bean plush toys, it is imperative that you protect them as carefully as possible. Follow the guidelines below to keep them in good condition.

1. Safeguard each swing tag by placing a tag protector over it. Tag protectors are clear acrylic sleeves that slide or fold over tags to keep them clean and unbent. This precaution is important because a missing, bent, creased, or dirty swing tag can drastically lower the value of a plush toy, decreasing it by as much as 50 percent or more.

2. Display or store plush toys in a dry, well-ventilated area to protect them from mold and mildew. If kept in a home with pets or smoke from tobacco, a fireplace, or a wood-burning stove, store plush toys in tightly sealed containers. Pet hair and smoke odor can significantly reduce the value. However, be sure that containers do not contain any moisture. Add desiccant to containers, if necessary.

3. Keep plush toys out of direct sunlight to prevent colors from fading.

4. Prevent dust from collecting on plush toys, especially on valuable or light-colored ones. Consider placing them in plastic display cases.

5. If you have a large, valuable collection, photograph it for insurance purposes. Also record the manufacturer, name, and price of each plush toy. These records will make filing a claim much easier in case of fire, flood, theft, or other loss. Keep a copy of your photos and inventory in a safe place.

Bits

Poochie Poo Key-Clip

Three variations of Liberty.

Bean Plush Variations

Mistakes are plush toys with errors that are inadvertently released to the public. They include misprints on tags, wrong tags, and errors in construction, such as missing limbs or features placed incorrectly.

Variations, on the other hand, are alterations that manufacturers intentionally make to popular bean plush styles. Variations most often incorporate changes in color, but they also include revisions in materials and other features.

Tag errors usually raise the value of plush toys only slightly because tags can be switched fairly easily with special equipment. Plush toys with construction errors are more valuable than those with tag errors. Variations are typically the most valuable because they are purposely produced in limited quantities of the most desired toys.

Two variations of Dad.

The Bean Plush Market

Where to Buy and Sell Bean Plush Toys

Collectors can buy from traditional stores, online, and from rummage sales. Each has distinct advantages and disadvantages.

TRADITIONAL STORES

Traditional stores, also known as "brick and mortar stores," are businesses where customers can physically enter and browse, as opposed to Internet shops where shoppers must go online to search for products.

Authorized Dealer Stores

Advantage: Authorized dealers are probably the most reliable retailers. It is very unlikely you will purchase a counterfeit plush toy from an authorized dealer. Also, authorized dealers typically sell only brand new products, and they normally have consistent prices. Furthermore, you can inspect each piece before buying it.

Disadvantage: Authorized dealers usually don't offer large discounts that can be found in other places, and they generally carry only the current plush toys of a single brand.

Secondary Stores

Secondary stores are businesses that do not buy directly from manufacturers or wholesalers.

Advantage: Secondary stores often carry multiple brands, as well as retired and hard-to-find plush toys. In addition, you can personally examine them before purchasing.

Disadvantage: Because dealers do not buy merchandise from manufacturers, you run a greater risk of purchasing counterfeit or flawed goods.

ONLINE

The Internet is the modern equivalent of the Old West, where law and order were sporadic at best. The Internet is expanding faster than law enforcement, so outlaws can rob innocent people and escape unscathed. Always be cautious when purchasing anything online.

Manufacturer Retail Sites

Advantage: Products sold by authorized dealers are virtually certain to be genuine and in pristine condition. Manufacturers guard their reputations zealously. Dealers who do not follow their strict rules risk losing their license to sell the company's products.

Disadvantage: Authorized dealers usually only carry a single brand because they have exclusive contracts with manufacturers who don't want their dealers selling competing brands. In addition, authorized dealers usually sell only current plush toys.

Secondary Store Sites

Advantage: Auction sites such as eBay, MetaExchange, and itradeBiz provide access to millions of people throughout the world at very low cost, thus eliminating the middleman. Savvy buyers can often find much lower prices than at retail outlets, and sellers can find buyers for virtually any new or used item.

Disadvantage: Auction sites create the most risk, as individual buyers and sellers may be inexperienced or dishonest. Also, buyers cannot inspect goods in person until after they have paid for them and received them in the mail. Plus, selling through an auction site takes considerable time and effort to determine appropriate pricing, describe items in detail, photograph them, keep records (including records for income taxes), communicate with potential buyers, answer questions, arrange payment, pack and mail items, and provide feedback. A major drawback of cutting out the middleman is that sellers assume much of the middleman's administrative work.

RUMMAGE SALES

Advantage: Rummage sales may well provide buyers the best opportunities to discover hidden treasures. Casual collectors who have lost interest in their plush toys often want to sell them with a minimum amount of time invested. A buyer can benefit when an uninformed seller offers a rare bean plush toy far below its real value. Another advantage of the rummage sale is that customers can personally inspect the items before paying and can ask any questions on the spot.

Disadvantage: People who hold rummage sales usually run them as "cash only, all sales final" transactions. Therefore, once you make your purchase, you will have little recourse if you later find you have purchased a plush toy that is not authentic.

Internet Resources

The following are Web sites that sell bean plush toys and/or provide information. Krause Publications is not affiliated with, nor does it endorse or guarantee the reliability of any of these sites. They are listed solely as a convenience to the collector.

Internet Auction Web Sites:

www.ebay.com (eBay)
www.metaexchange.com (MetaExchange)
www.addiesattic.com (Addie's Attic)

Manufacturer's Web Sites:

www.cavanaghgrp.com (Coca-Cola)
www.swibco.com (Puffkins)
www.ty.com (Ty)
www.webkinz.com (Webkinz)
www.shiningstars.com (Shining Stars)
www.disney.go.com/shopping (Disney)
www.liquidblue.com (Grateful Dead)
www.wbshop.com (Warner Brothers)

Online Community Data Base:

www.stashmatic.com

Authentication:

www.truebluebeans.com

www.pbbags.com

www.beaniephenomenon.com

Online Bean Plush Information:

www.shopoli.com
www.toniscollectibles.com
www.theturtletrail.com
www.debiscollectibles.com
www.awarenessribbonbears.com
www.traderlist.com
www.2collectcola.com
www.aboutbeanies.com
www.msjanie.com
www.randyandtheresa.com
www.beaniephenomenon.com
www.doodlespage.com
www.salsattic.com
www.smartcollecting.com
www.bbtoystore.com
www.beanwatcher.com
www.kimskornercc.com
www.shiningstars.com
www.beanieuniverse.com

Ty Hang Tag and Tush Tag Identification

Introduction

The value of a Ty bean plush toy is greatly affected by the version (generation) of its tags. Thus, being able to accurately identify its tags is essential to determining its value.

Each Ty plush toy has two tags—a hang tag and a tush tag. The hang tag is a heart-shaped cardboard tag attached to the toy with a plastic fastener. The tag is sometimes called a swing tag because it swings loosely from its fastener. The tush tag is a cloth tag bearing manufacturing information that is sewn into the seam.

A number of hang tag and tush tag variations, known as generations, have been used. Variations exist within generations and a number of special variations have been made as well. This guide does not cover all versions of tags but focuses on the most widely distributed ones.

We have included photos and descriptions to help you identify them.

Hang Tag Condition Grading Scale

A plush toy's hang tag accounts for as much as 50 percent of its value, so it's essential that buyers and sellers use a common grading scale to prevent misunderstanding. The following grades form the accepted standard for describing the condition of a bean plush tag.

Mint: The tag is in perfect condition with no creases, bends, tears, spider veins, scratches, dents, smudges, or price stickers.

Near Mint: The tag is in almost perfect condition. It may have a slight dent or scratch but no crease. Valued at 80 to 90 percent of mint.

Excellent: The tag may have a slight crease or other minor defect. Valued at 70 to 80 percent of mint.

Very Good: The tag may have a significant crease or other defect but is whole. Valued at 60 to 70 percent of mint.

Good: The tag may have several defects, including tears or large creases. Valued at 50 to 60 percent of mint.

Poor: The tag has a number of defects. Valued less than 50 percent of mint.

Ty Beanie Baby Hang Tags

The Beanie Babies™ Collection
Humphrey™ -Style 4060
®1993 Ty Inc. Oakbrook, IL USA
All Rights Reseved. Caution
Remove this tag before giving
toy to a child For ages 5 and up
Handmade in China
Surface
Wash

First Generation

The first generation tag is a single tag and doesn't open like a book. The front of the tag is red with a gold border and "TY" printed on the center in thin white letters. On the back are the Beanie's name and style number, copyright, care information, and the country of manufacture.

Note: Produced with 1st Generation Tush Tag.

Second Generation

The most common second generation tags feature a bar code and the words, "Retain Tag For Reference" on the back. Copyright and care information appear on the left inside section. The right inside section shows the Beanie's name, style number, and the words "to," "from," and "with love."

Note: Produced with 1st Generation Tush Tag.

Third Generation

The most prevalent third generation tags feature a heart with slightly rounder shape and larger, rounder "TY" letters on the front. On the inside left panel, a trademark symbol appears after "Beanie Babies" in the header. Below the header, three corporate addresses are listed with a copyright symbol before each. Above the bar code on the back is a warning to remove swing tags before giving to a child.

Note: Produced with 1st and 2nd Generation Tush Tags.

Fourth Generation

Fourth generation tags feature a yellow star on the front containing the words "ORIGINAL BEANIE BABY" and a slightly smaller TY logo. Also new to this tag are the Beanie's birth date, a poem, the words "Visit our web page!!!," and http://www.ty.com, all printed on the inside right page. Because of a temporary legal dispute over the domain name, on some tags the Web address was cut off or covered with a sticker.

Note: Produced with 3rd, 4th, and 5th Generation Tush Tags.

Fifth Generation

The outside of this tag (bearing the bar code and Ty logo) is virtually the same as that of the fourth generation, but all lettering on the tag now uses the Comic Sans font. On the inside left page, the trademark symbol in the header has been replaced with the registered symbol. On the inside right page, the Beanie's birth date is spelled out, the style number and the words "Visit our web page" have been deleted, and the Web address has been shortened to "www.ty.com."

Note: Produced with 6th, 7th, and 8th Generation Tush Tags.

Sixth Generation

On the front of the sixth generation tags, a holographic star marked with "2000" replaces the yellow star. Four distribution locations are listed on the left inside page. On the right inside page, the Beanie's name, birth date, and a poem are written in smaller letters. A smaller bar code and a revised safety warning appears on the back.

Note: Produced with 9th Generation Tush Tags.

Seventh Generation

This tag is found on Beanies released in the U.K. It displays three significant changes from the sixth generation tags. First, the word "BEANIES" rather than "2000" is written across the star on the front. Second, "Gosport (or Gasport) P013 OFP" appears beneath the "Ty Europe" listing. And third, the wording of the safety warning has been revised. All European tags have "BEANIES" rather than "BEANIE BABIES" on the front of the tags.

Note: Produced with 9th, 10th, 11th, and 12th Generation Tush Tags.

Eighth Generation

Eighth generation tags are essentially the same as sixth generation tags, except that on the front, the words "BEANIE BABY" are written in a circle around the holographic star.

Note: Produced with 8th Generation Tush Tags.

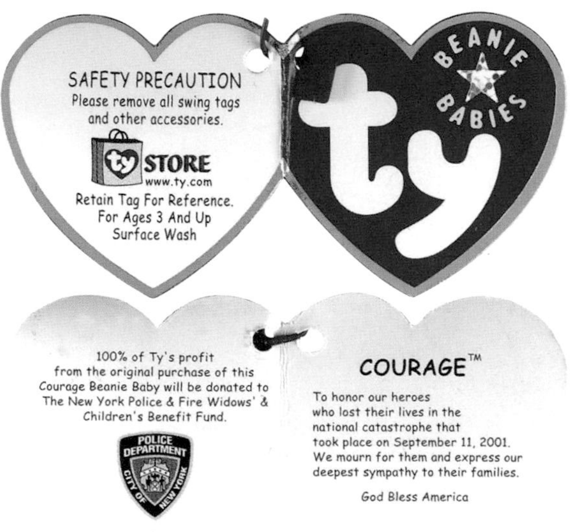

Ninth Generation

These tags are almost identical to eighth generation tags. The one slight change is that on the front "BEANIE BABY" is now plural, so it reads, "BEANIE BABIES" instead.

Note: Produced with 10th Generation Tush Tags.

Tenth Generation

Tenth generation tags feature a significant change to the front of the tag. The single holographic star is replaced by five holographic stars above the words, "BEANIE BABIES," which are printed in a curve above the "Y" in "TY."

Note: Produced with 11th Generation Tush Tags.

Eleventh Generation

To commemorate the ten-year anniversary of Beanie Babies, the five holographic stars on the front of the tag are replaced by a holographic number "10" and a white star with the abbreviation "yrs" surrounded by a holographic starburst pattern. On the inside left page, the words "Handmade in China" are deleted, and six distribution locations are listed in two columns.

Note: Produced with 12th, and 13th Generation Tush Tags.

Twelfth Generation

"Original" has been added over the word "BEANIE" and a comet has been added underneath.

Note: Produced with 13th Generation Tush Tags.

Thirteenth Generation

The comet has been removed and a star added next to the left of the prhase "Beanie Babies."

Note: Produced with 13th Generation Tush Tags.

Fourteenth Generation

The star has been changed to yellow and is placed behind the word "ORIGINAL."

Note: Produced with 13th Generation Tush Tags.

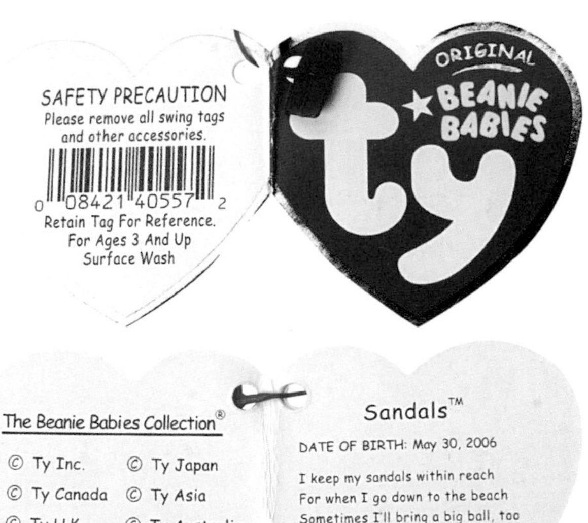

Fifteenth Generation

The star has been removed and a slash placed below the word "ORIGINAL."

Note: Produced with 13th Generation Tush Tags.

UK Tags

Ty UK tags have changed with the generations of USA tags, with the exception of having only the word "Beanies" on the tag rather than "Beanie Babies." 14th generation tag shown.

Beanie Babies Special Hang Tags

There are some tags for special occasions within the Beanie Babies line. For example, the 12th generation tag on page 40 is for Wildlife Fund toys offered on the Ty Web site.

Ty Beanie Baby Special Hang Tags

Alphabet Beanies

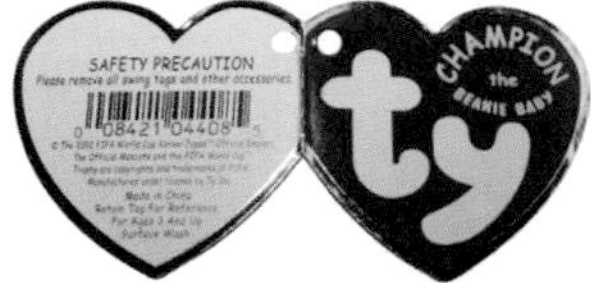

Champion

Charity (For the Cure)

Beanie Baby of the Month

Decade

Happy Birthday (large)

New Original 9

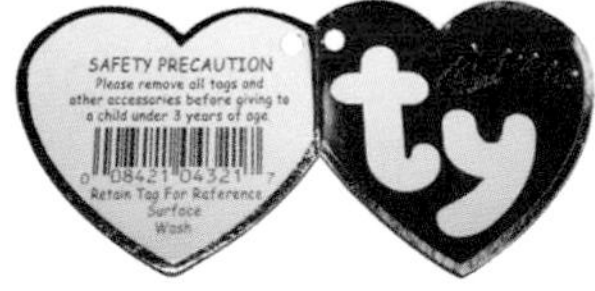

Zodiac

Beanie Babies 2.0

The Beanie Babies 2.0 introduced in 2008 display a holographic "Ty" on the front of their hang tag. The plastic fastener is attached to the outside of the tag to hide the secret code that allows the buyer to access special activities on the designated Web site.

Ty Hang Tags - Other Lines

Each of the Ty lines has a unique hang tag. Most of the tags are variations of the 15th generation noted previously. The original tags were a single heart with a front and back but no fold. Most tags are folded now, with the exception of the Bow Wow and Teenie Beanie Babies lines.

Angeline

Attic Treasures

Attic Treasures
5th and 6th Generation

Baby Ty

Basket Beanies

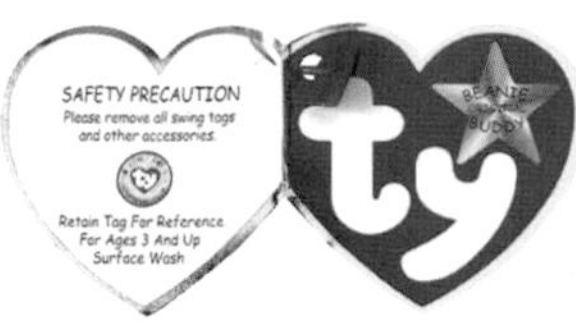

Beanie Buddies

Bow Wow (single sided - does not fold)

Beanie Boppers

Beanie Kids

Classic

Ty Girlz

Halloweenies

Jingle Beanies

Pillow Pals

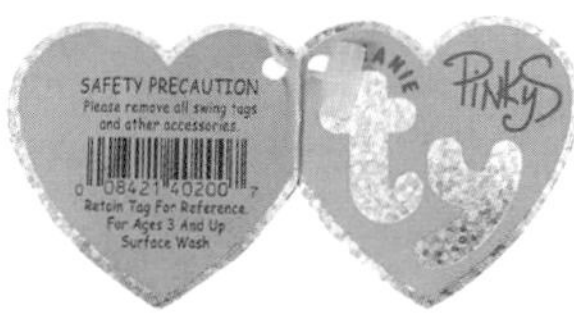

Pinkys

Pluffies

Punkies

Teenie Beanie Babies
(single sided - does not fold)

Teenie Beanie Boppers

Valenteenies

Ty Tush Tags

© 1993 TY INC.,
OAKBROOK IL. U. S. A.
ALL RIGHTS RESERVED
HANDMADE IN CHINA
SURFACE WASHABLE

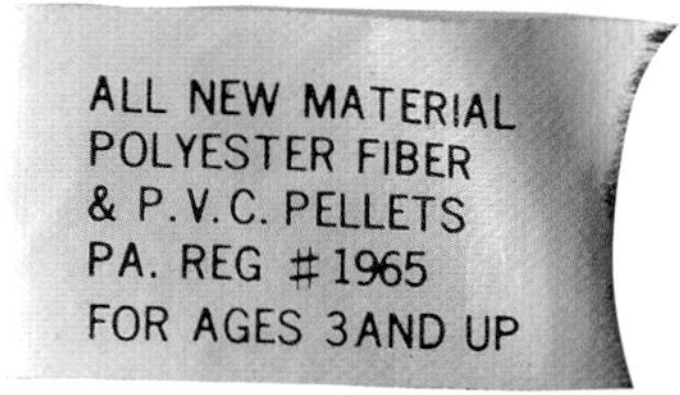

ALL NEW MATERIAL
POLYESTER FIBER
& P. V. C. PELLETS
PA. REG #1965
FOR AGES 3AND UP

First Generation

This looped, black-and-white tag is printed with either a 1993 or 1995 copyright date, and lists the country of origin as China or Korea. The tag does not include the Beanie's name, and some tags do not have the CE symbol (Conformite Europeenne) or the words, "FOR AGES 3 AND UP."

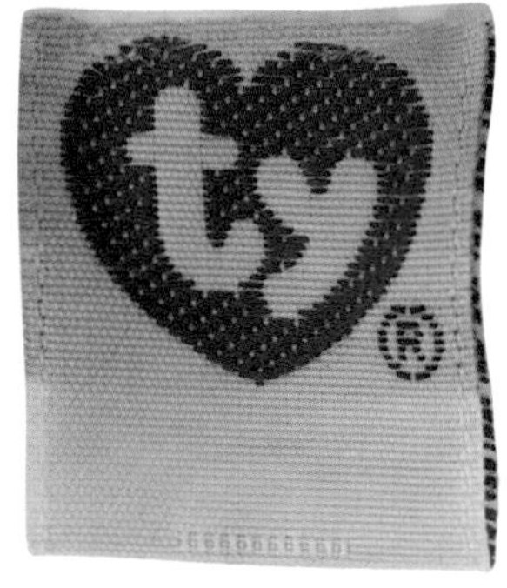

Second Generation

This tag features a large red heart with a white Ty logo in the center and a registered mark below and to the right. Like the first generation tag, the tags display the 1993 or 1995 copyright date, and a Korean or Chinese origin. Also, the Beanie name is not included, and some tags do not carry the "FOR AGES 3 AND UP" statement.

Third Generation

The most significant change in this tag is the much smaller heart size, the inclusion of the Beanie's name at the bottom, and the phrase, "The Beanie Babies Collection" at the top.

Fourth Generation

The first fourth generation tush tags were actually third generation tags that carried a sticker with a small red star placed to the left of the heart. Later fourth generation tags had stars printed directly on the tag.

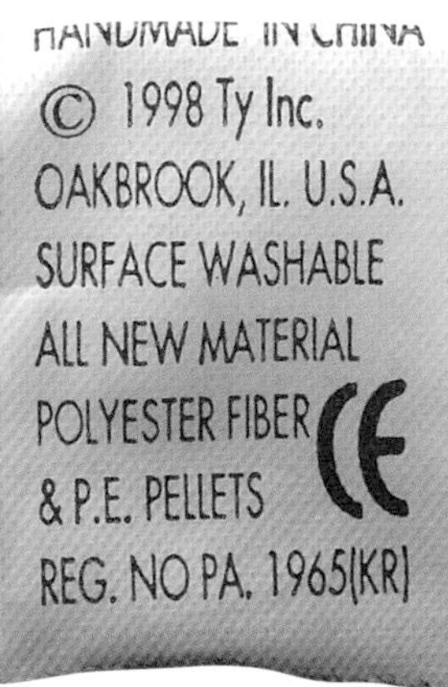

Fifth Generation

This tag displays a registered symbol after the words "Beanie Babies" at the top of the tag. Also, the trademark symbol is added after the Beanie name at the bottom of the tag.

Sixth Generation

On sixth generation tags, a single registered symbol in the line "THE BEANIE BABIES COLLECTION" replaces the trademark and registered symbols found in this line in the fifth generation tag. The tags may list either P.E. or P.V.C. pellets as fillings, and some versions feature a red or purple Chinese stamp inside the loop to identify the factory in which the Beanie was manufactured.

Seventh Generation

This generation tag features a hologram displaying a heart and the words, "The BEANIE BABIES Collection." The heart is printed with heat-sensitive disappearing ink to make counterfeiting even more difficult. None of the loops contain Chinese stamps.

Eighth Generation

Eighth generation tags are identical to seventh generation tags, except that they are no longer made as loops.

HANDMADE IN CHINA
© 2000 TY INC.,
OAKBROOK, IL. U.S.A.
SURFACE WASHABLE
ALL NEW MATERIAL
POLYESTER FIBER
& P.E. PELLETS
REG.NO PA 1965(KR)

Ninth Generation

The looped tag returned with the ninth generation. Inside the loop is an eight character code comprised of a combination of letters and numbers. Within the hologram, "BEANIE" appears above and "BABIES" below the heart, with alternating "TY" and star images inside the heart. In addition, small stars and hearts surround the central image.

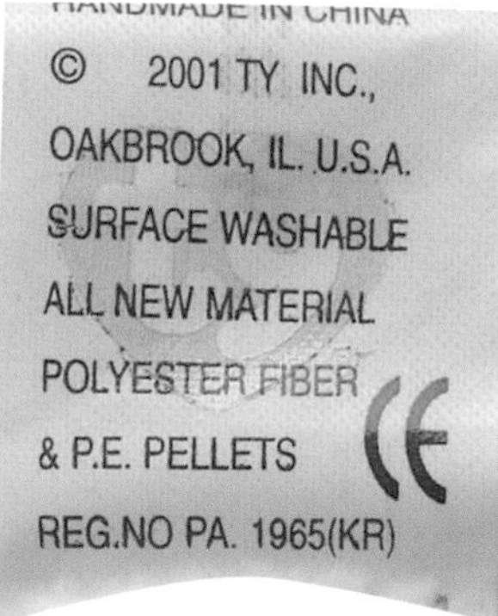

Tenth Generation

In this tag, concentric hearts surround the main heart and "TY" image, while "Beanie Babies" is printed in a repeated diagonal pattern in the background.

Eleventh Generation

The main image in the eleventh generation hologram is an alternating Beanie Bear and Ty heart logo. The background is filled with various sized hearts and stars.

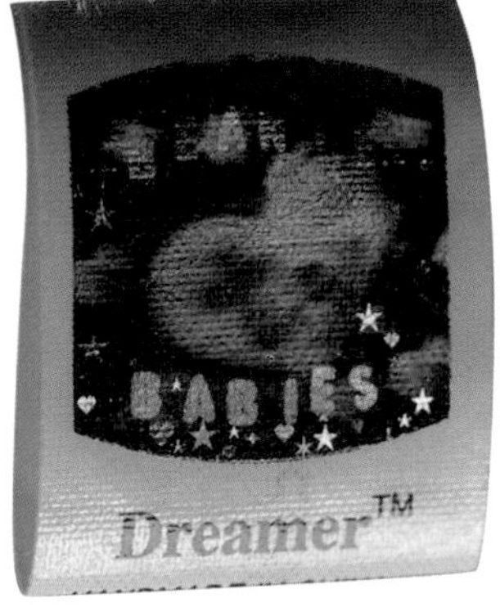

HANDMADE IN CHINA
© 2002 TY INC.,
OAKBROOK, IL. U.S.A.
SURFACE WASHABLE
ALL NEW MATERIAL
POLYESTER FIBER
& P.E. PELLETS CE
REG.NO PA. 1965(KR)

Twelfth Generation

In the twelfth generation, the Ty heart logo is tilted and off center, and the stars and hearts in the background are smaller. Some tags have a much larger CE symbol on the back.

Thirteenth Generation

After creating a series of increasingly complex tush tags, Ty returned to a simpler design resembling its second-generation tag. However, the thirteenth generation still uses a shiny red foil heart and retains the Beanie's name at the bottom.

Not to be removed until
delivered to the consumer

This label is affixed in compliance
with the Upholstered and
Stuffed Articles Act

This article contains
NEW MATERIAL ONLY

Made by Ont. Reg. No.
20B6484

Content: Plastic Pellets
Polyester Fibers

Made in China

Ne pas enlever avant livraison
au consommateur

Cette étiquette est apposée
conformément à loi sur
les articles rembourrés

Cet article contient
MATÉRIAU NEUF SEULEMENT

Fabriqué par No d'enrg.Ont.
20B6484

Contenu: Boulette de plastique
Fibres de Polyester

Fabriqué en Chine

Canadian

Beanies sold in Canada have an additional tag to meet Canadian regulations. The tag is printed in both English and French.

Explanation of Listings

Name: The official name of the plush toy.

Style: The style number of the plush toy.

Bday: Beanie Babies and some of the other lines include a birthday.

Intro: The date on which the plush toy was introduced or released for sale.

Gen: The generation number of the tag. Each generation represents a tag that is different than the previous one.

$: The current average value of the plush toy.

Note: Specific information referring to a description of the plush toy. Also, the exclusive event or location where the plush toy is or was sold or a variation in manufacturing.

Ty Angeline

Holiday Angeline, Angeline Book, Angeline

This is the only Ty line that features just a single character. Angeline is a precious little angel doll who tells her story in her own book, *A Story of Love.* Besides the original doll dressed in a blue gown, she has other colored gowns: pink for Valentine's Day, yellow for spring, and red for the holidays. She comes in different sizes, including a 3" doll key-clip. She has two gift bags and a story book. Some dolls come boxed.

Spring Angeline

Name	Style	Intro	Gen	$	Note
Angeline	63001	3/4/05	1	8	blue dress
Angeline Book	66000	3/4/05	1	8	
Angeline Key-clip	63008	3/4/05	1	6	blue dress
Gift Bag	63010	3/4/05	none	4	w/tissue
Happy Birthday	63006	3/4/05	1	8	boxed blue dress
Happy Holidays	63019	9/30/05	2	8	boxed red dress
Happy Valentine's Day	63028	12/30/05	2	8	boxed pink dress
Holiday Angeline	63018	9/30/05	2	8	red dress
Holiday Angeline	63018	9/30/05	2	15	red dress, large
Holiday Angeline Key-clip	63020	9/30/05	2	6	red dress
Holiday Gift Bag	63021	9/30/05	none	4	w/tissue

Valentine Angeline

Name	Style	Intro	Gen	$	Note
I Love You	63003	3/4/05	1	8	boxed blue dress
Just for You	63005	3/4/05	1	8	boxed blue dress
Spring Angeline	63035	4/28/06	2	8	yellow dress
Spring Angeline	63036	3/4/05	2	15	yellow dress, large
Spring Angeline	63037	4/28/06	2	8	You're An Angel
To Cheer You	63002	3/4/05	1	8	boxed blue dress
Valentine Angeline	63026	12/30/05	2	8	pink dress
Valentine Angeline	63030	12/30/05	2	15	pink dress, large
You Are Special	63007	3/4/05	1	8	boxed blue dress
You're An Angel	63004	3/4/05	1	8	boxed blue dress

Ty Attic Treasures

Top Row: Calliope, William, Alfalfa
Bottom Row: Breezy, Scarlet, Ramsey, Bugsy

Ty introduced the first twelve Attic Treasures in 1993 and produced more than 230 different animals plus variations through 2002. Unlike Ty's other creations, Attic Treasures feature moveable joints. They vary in size from 6" to 20" and many include clothing and accessories. All Attic Treasures are retired, which increases their value.

Allura

Azure

Name	Style	Intro	Gen	$	Note
Abby	6027	1995	2, 3	65, 30	w/overalls, 2G +ribbon: $80
Abby	6027	1995	4, 5, 6	10, 8, 10	w/overalls
Abby	6027	1995	2, 3, 4	50, 20, 15	w/ribbon
Adeliade	6262	1/1/01	7	5	
Alfalfa	6241	8/27/00	7	5	
Allura	6058	4/14/99	7	5	
Amethyst	6131	1/1/98	6	10	
Amore	6206	7/4/00	7	5	
April	6268	1/1/01	7	5	
Arlene	6260	1/1/01	7	5	
Armstrong	6226	6/24/00	7	5	
Azalea	6093	1/1/99	7	5	
Azure	6055	4/20/99	7	5	
Babette	6263	4/26/01	7	5	
Baron	6225	6/24/00	7	5	

Beezee

Blarney

Name	Style	Intro	Gen	$	Note
Barry	6073	1997	5	30	
Barrymore	6288	12/27/01	7	5	
Basil	6284	8/27/00	7	7	
Beargundy	6205	8/31/99	7	5	
Bearington	6102	1/1/98	6	6	
Bearkhardt	6204	8/31/99	7	5	
Beezee	6088	1/1/99	7	5	
Benjamin	6023	1995	2*, 2, 5	30*, 25, 15	*w/ribbon, w/sweater
Berkley	6218	1/4/00	7	5	
Beverly	6210	1/4/00	7	5	
Birch	6232	7/16/00	7	5	
Blarney	6215	1/4/00	7	5	
Bloom	6122	1/1/98	6	10	
Bluebeary	6080	1/1/98	6, 7	5, 5	
Blush	6208	1/4/00	7	5	

Carson

Casanova

Name	Style	Intro	Gen	$	Note
Bonnie	6075	1/1/98	6, 7	5, 5	
Boris	6041	1996/97	5	20, 20	no clothes, w/sweater
Breezy	6057	4/21/99	7	5	
Brewster	6034	1995	2, 3, 4, 5	12, 10, 8, 5	w/overalls
Brewster	6034	1995	2, 3, 4,	12, 10, 8,	no clothes
Brisbane	6052	4/20/99	7	5	
Buck	6281	9/3/01	7	5	
Bugsy	6089	1/1/99	7	5	
Burrows	6291	12/27/01	7	5	
Caboose	6267	6/23/01	7	5	
Calliope	6230	6/24/00	7	5	
Camelia	6094	1/1/99	7	5	
Carey	6284	1/1/01	7	5	
Carlisle	6279	9/3/01	7	5	
Carlton	6064	1996	5	45, 30	w/ribbon, w/overalls

Checkers

Cheri

Name	Style	Intro	Gen	$	Note
Carmella	6280	6/23/01	7	5	
Carmichael	6282	6/23/01	7	5	
Carson	6216	1/4/00	7	5	
Carver	6271	9/3/01	7	5	
Casanova	6073	1/1/98	6, 7	6, 5	
Cassandra	6249	1/1/01	7	5	
Cassia	6306	6/22/02	7	5	
Cassie	6028	1995	2, 3, 4, 5	55, 35, 18, 7	w/jumper, 4G +ribbon: $55
Cassie	6028	1995	2, 3, 4	60, 45, 30	w/ribbon
Cawley	6090	1/1/99	7	5	
Charles	6039	1996	5	25, 25	no clothes, w/overalls
Checkers	6031	1995	2, 3, 4	35, 25, 14	no clothes
Checkers	6031	1995	5, 6, 7	14, 5, 5	no clothes
Checkers	6031	1995	2, 3, 5	40, 45, 7	w/sweater

Darlene

Dexter

Name	Style	Intro	Gen	$	Note
Chelsea	6070	1996	5, 6	5, 5	
Cheri	6200	8/31/99	7	5	
Chillings	6286	10/1/01	7	5	
Christopher	6071	1996	5, 6	5	
Clay	6233	6/24/00	7	5	
Clifford	6003	1993/96	1	90, 200	
Clyde	6040	1996	5	20	
Cody	6030	1995	2, 3, 4	40, 30, 10	
Cody	6030	1995	5, 6, 7	5, 5, 5	
Colby	6043	1996	5	16, 13, 13*	no clothes, *w/jumper
Cooper	6251	1/1/01	7	5	
Copperfield	6060	1996	5	20	
Cromwell	6221	1/4/00	7	5	
Dad	6297	3/29/02	7	5	
Darlene	6213	1/4/00	7	5	

Fairbanks

Fairchild

Name	Style	Intro	Gen	$	Note
Demetria	6307	6/22/02	7	5	
Devlin	6277	9/3/01	7	5	
Dexter	6009	1993	4, 5	20, 13	
Dexter	6009	1993	1, 2, 4, 5	50, 65, 20, 25	
Dexter	6009	1993	4, 5	15, 7	
Dickens	6038	1995	4, 5, 6	12, 6, 5	no clothes
Dickens	6038	1995	4, 5, 6	25, 6, 5	w/overalls
Digby	6013	1994	1	210	w/ribbon & humpback
Digby	6013	1994	1, 4, 5	90, 65, 90	w/ribbon & straight back
Digby	6013	1994	4, 5	50, 22	w/sweater
Domino	6042	1996	5	25, 25	no clothes, w/overalls
Easton	6042	6/24/00	7	5	
Ebony	6130	1/1/98	6	11	w/jumper
Ebony	6130	1996	5	15	w/jumper

Franny

Gordon

Name	Style	Intro	Gen	$	Note
Elizabeth	6261	6/23/01	7	5	
Emily	6016	1994	1	120	w/bow & large feet
Emily	6016	1994	1, 3, 4, 5	90, 60, 40, 70	w/bow & small feet
Emily	6016	1994	1, 3, 4, 5	175, 90, 75, 35	w/hat & dress
Emma	6299	4/30/02	7	5	
Emmet	6253	1/1/01	7	5	
Esmerelda	6086	9/30/98	6, 7	6, 5	
Eva	6276	6/23/01	7	5	
Eve	6106	5/30/98	6, 7	6, 5	
Fairbanks	6059	4/21/99	7	5	
Fairchild	6220	1/4/00	7	5	
Fern	6235	6/24/00	7	5	
Fields	6292	12/27/01	7	5	

Gwyndolyn

Hayes

Name	Style	Intro	Gen	$	Note
Flannigan	6296	12/27/01	7	5	
Fleecia	6293	12/27/01	7	5	
Flynn	6287	12/27/01	7	5	
Franny	6229	6/24/00	7	5	
Fraser	6010	1993	1, 2, 4, 5	60, 40, 16, 18	w/ribbon
Fraser	6010	1993	1	95	w/ribbon & artist tag
Fraser	6010	1993	5, 6	6, 5	w/sweater
Frederick	6072	1996	5	18	
Gem	6107	9/30/98	7	6	
Genevieve	6274	4/26/01	7	8	
Georgette	6091	1/1/99	7	5	
Georgia	6095	1/1/99	7	5	
Gilbert Gold	6006	1993	1, 5	70, 5	w/overalls
Gilbert Gold	6006	1993	1	80	w/ribbon

Ivan

Klause

Name	Style	Intro	Gen	$	Note
Gilbert White	6015	1993	1	200	
Gloria	6123	5/30/98	6	11	
Gordon	6110	1/1/99	7	6	
Grace	6142	1/1/98	6	5	
Grady	6051	1995	5	40	
Grant	6101	1/1/98	6, 7	7, 6	
Greyson	6234	7/16/00	7	5, 5	long fur, short fur
Grover	6050	1995	5	12	brown w/overalls
Grover	6050	1995	2, 3	45, 30	w/ribbon, w/overalls +ribbon
Grover	6050	1/1/98	6	10	brown w/overalls
Grover	6050	1995	2, 3, 4	25, 18, 18	brown w/ribbon
Grover Gold	6051	1995	5	19	w/sweater
Grover Gold	6051	1995	4, 5	20, 25	no clothes w/ribbon
Gwyndolyn	6209	8/31/99	7	5	

Lawrence

Marigold

Name	Style	Intro	Gen	$	Note
Hagatha	6273	9/3/01	7	5	
Harper	6214	1/4/00	7	5	
Hayes	6212	1/4/00	7	5	
Heartley	6111	1/1/99	7	5	
Heather	6061	1996	5	24	w/overalls , +ribbon: $90
Heather	6061	1996	5	55	no clothes +ribbon
Henry Brown	6005	1994	1, 5	80, 12	w/overalls, 1G +ribbon: $110
Henry Brown	6005	1994	1	50	w/ribbon
Henry Gold	6005	1993	1	320	
Hogan	6245	1/1/01	7	5	
Hutchins	6290	12/27/01	7	5	
Iris	6077	1/1/98	6, 7	5, 5	
Isabella	6109	9/30/98	7	6	
Ivan	6029	1995	2, 3, 4	70, 55, 18	

Merwyn

Mulligan

Name	Style	Intro	Gen	$	Note
Ivan	6029	1995	5, 6, 7	6, 5, 5	
Ivory	6062	1996	5	120, 17	no clothes w/ribbon, w/overalls
Ivy	6076	1/1/98	6, 7	5, 5	
Jack	6989	1998	6, 7	9, 8	UK
Jangle	6082	9/30/98	7	5	
Jeremy	6008	1993	1, 2, 4, 5	75, 35, 28, 35	no clothes w/ ribbon
Jeremy	6008	1993	4, 5	45, 20	w/sweater
Jeremy	6008	1993	2, 4, 5, 5*	70, 50, 65, 15*	w/sweater & ribbon, *w/ overalls
Justin	6044	1996	5	65	
Kaiser	6265	4/26/01	7	5	
Karena	6301	4/30/02	7	5	
Katrina	6054	4/22/99	7	5	
King	6140	1/1/98	6	18	

Peppermint

Peter

Name	Style	Intro	Gen	$	Note
King	6140	1996	5, 5	20, 20	no clothes, w/cape
Kingston	6236	6/24/00	7	5	
Klause	6239	8/27/00	7	5	
Kyoto	6603	10/18/01	7	8	
Lancaster	6289	12/27/01	7	5	
Laurel	6081	9/30/98	7	5	
Lawrence	6053	4/20/99	7	5	
Lilly	6037	1995	2, 3, 4	80, 65, 40	w/jumper
Lilly	6037	1995	5, 6	7, 5	w/jumper
Lilly	6037	1995	2, 3, 4	100, 85, 55	w/jumper & ribbon
Lilly	6037	1995	2, 3, 4	65, 45, 40	w/ribbon
Logan	6602	10/1/01	7	8	
Mackenzie	6999	1998	6, 7	28, 22	Canada - 7G Patriot tag: $35
Madison	6035	1995	2, 3, 4	55, 45, 7, 5	w/overalls

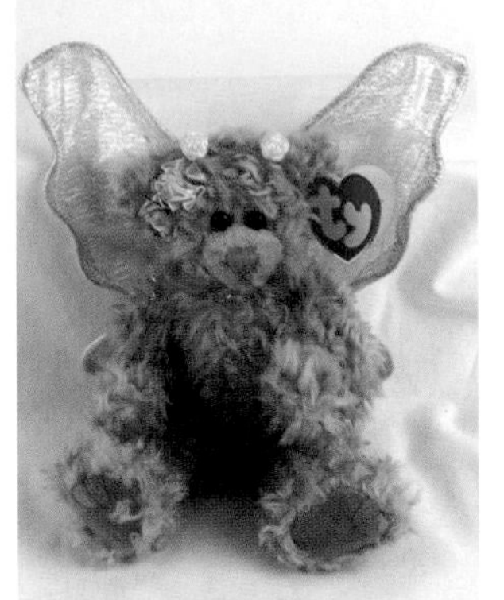

Rafaella

Ramsey

Name	Style	Intro	Gen	$	Note
Madison	6035	1995	5, 6	35*, 7, 5	*w/overalls & ribbon, w/overalls
Madison	6035	1995	2, 3, 4	25, 25, 25	no clothes w/ribbon
Majesty	6259	6/23/01	7	6	
Malcolm	6112	4/20/99	7	6	
Malcolm	6026	1995	2, 3, 4, 5	60, 55, 25, 20	w/sweater, 4G +ribbon: $45
Malcolm	6026	1995	2, 3, 4,	50, 40, 30	no clothes w/ribbon
Marigold	6228	6/24/00	7	5	
Martina	6303	4/30/02	7	5	
Mason	6020	1995	2, 4, 5	40, 25, 22	w/ribbon
Mason	6020	1995	4, 5, 6	35, 6, 5	w/sweater, 4G +ribbon: $45
Max	6246	8/27/00	7	6	
May	6256	1/1/01	7	5	
McKinley	6604	1/27/02	7	5	

Rosalie

Salty

Name	Style	Intro	Gen	$	Note
Mei Li	6272	6/23/01	7	5	
Merwyn	6243	8/27/00	7	5	
Minerva	6247	1/1/01	7	5	
Mom	6270	3/3/01	7	7	
Mommy	6298	3/29/02	7	5	
Montgomery	6143	1/1/98	6	7	
Morgan	6018	1994	1	52	
Morgan	6018	1994	5, 6	6, 5	
Mrs. Santabear	6285	10/1/01	7	5	
Mulligan	6231	6/24/00	7	5	
Murphy	6033	1995	2, 3, 4	18, 18, 18	no clothes
Murphy	6033	1995	2, 3, 4, 5	17, 17, 17, 6	w/overalls
Nicholas	6015	1994	1, 4	120, 140	w/ribbon
Nicholas	6015	1994	5, 6, 7	6, 5, 20	w/sweater

Skylar

Susannah

Name	Style	Intro	Gen	$	Note
Nola	6014	1994	1, 5	110*, 155, 45	*w/ ribbon, w/hat & dress
Nola	6014	1994	1, 2, 3, 4, 5	130, 110, 90, 70, 80	no clothes w/bow
North	6244	8/27/00	7	5	
Olivia	6258	1/1/01	7	5	
Olympia	6308	6/22/02	7	5	
Orion	6207	9/31/99	7	5	
Oscar	6025	1995	2, 3, 4, 5, 6	35, 22, 16, 7, 6	w/overalls
Oscar	6025	1995	2, 3, 4	28, 20, 20	w/ribbon
Penelope	6036	1995	2, 3, 4	28, 22, 20	no clothes
Penelope	6036	1995	4, 5	34, 12	w/overalls
Peppermint	6074	1/1/98	6, 7	6, 5	
Peter	6084	9/30/98	7	5	

Tyrone

Washington

Name	Style	Intro	Gen	$	Note
Peter aka Pumpkin	6084	9/30/98	6	7	
Piccadilly	6069	5/30/98	6, 7	6, 5	blue & green
Piccadilly	6069	5/30/98	7	5	multicolored
Piccadilly	6069	6/1/98	6	7	small bear hang tag
Piccadilly	6069	6/1/98	7	8	Azalea hang tag
Pouncer	6011	1994	6, 7	5, 5	w/jumper
Pouncer	6011	1994	1, 3	170, 60	w/ribbon & different colored ears
Pouncer	6011	1994	1	60	w/ribbon & same colored ears
Pouncer	6011	1994	5	6	w/sweater
Precious	6104	1/1/98	6	6	
Prince	6048	1996	6, 7	7, 6	
Priscilla	6045	1996	5	20*, 15	*w/no clothes, w/overalls
Purrcy	6022	1995	6, 7	5, 5	w/jumper

Weatherby

William

Name	Style	Intro	Gen	$	Note
Purrcy	6022	1995	5	5	w/overalls
Purrcy	6022	1995	5	65, 60, 40, 30	w/ribbon
Radcliffe	6087	1/1/99	7	5	
Rafaella	6066	4/9/99	7	5	
Ramsey	6092	1/1/99	7	5	
Rebecca	6019	1995	2, 4, 5	175, 90, 35	w/overalls & red bow
Rebecca	6019	1995	2, 4, 5	75, 55, 75	w/overalls & blue bow
Reggie	6004	1993	1	110	w/Hong Kong hang tag
Reggie	6004	1993	1	95	w/Korea hang tag
Revere	6305	4/30/02	7	5	
Rhine	6601	8/25/01	7	7	
River	6237	6/24/00	7	5	
Rosalie	6068	4/22/99	7	5	
Rosalyne	6211	1/4/00	7	5	

Name	Style	Intro	Gen	$	Note
Rose	6078	1/1/98	6, 7	5, 5	
Salty	6056	4/22/99	7	5	
Samuel	6105	5/30/98	6, 7	6, 5	
Samuel aka Large Bear	6105	5/30/98	6	6	
Santabear	6284	10/1/01	7	5	
Sara	6120	1/1/98	6, 7	7, 6	
Sara	6120	1993	5, 5, 4	55*, 12, 45	*w/ribbon
Sara	6120	1993	1, 2, 3, 4, 5	80, 70, 45, 30, 40	w/ribbon, 1G w/artist tush tag: $210
Scarlet	6224	6/24/00	7	5	
Scooter	6032	1995	2	20	no clothes
Scooter	6032	1995	2, 5	20, 20	w/sweater
Scotch	6103	1/1/98	6, 7	10, 22	
Scruffy	6085	1/1/98	6	5	coarse, tacked ears
Scruffy	6085	1/1/98	6, 7	5, 5	plush floppy ears
Shelby	6024	1995	2, 5, 6	40, 7, 6	w/dress
Shelby	6024	1995	2	30	w/ribbon
Sidney	6121	1/1/98	6	8	
Sire	6141	1/1/98	6	6	
Skylar	6096	1/1/99	7	5, 6	w/black nose, w/rust nose
Socrates	6269	3/30/01	7	6	
Sophia	6278	4/26/01	7	6	
Spencer	6046	1996	5	16, 14	no clothes, w/sweater
Spruce	6203	8/31/99	7	10	
Squeaky	6017	1994	1, 5, 6	70, 6, 5	
Squeaky	6017	1994	1	60, 55	w/clr, w/blk whiskers
Sterling	6083	9/30/98	7	6, 5	w/7" wings, w/6" wings
Strawbunny	6079	1/1/98	6, 7	5, 5	
Suki	6266	1/1/01	7	5	
Surprise	6311	6/22/02	7	5	
Susannah	6067	4/17/99	7	5	

Name	Style	Intro	Gen	$	Note
Tiny Tim	6001	1993	2, 4, 5	50, 35, 8	w/overalls
Tiny Tim	6001	1993	2, 4, 5,	55, 30, 55	w/overalls & ribbon
Tiny Tim	6001	1993	1, 2, 4, 5	65, 45, 20, 35	w/ribbon
Tracey	6047	1996	5	18, 16	no clothes, w/overalls
Tracey	6047	1996	5	16	
Tudor	6600	9/2/01	7	9	
Tyler	6002	1993	1	140	humpback w/ ribbon
Tyler	6002	1993	1	85, 40, 40, 30	Straight back w/darker nose
Tyler	6002	1993	2, 4, 5	65, 30, 18	w/sweater
Tyler	6002	1993	1, 2, 4	100, 80, 50	w/sweater & ribbon
Tyra	6201	8/31/99	7	500, 165	w/pompoms, no pompoms
Tyrone	6108	9/30/98	7	5	
Uncle Sam	6257	4/26/01	7	6	
Vlad	6275	9/3/01	7	5	
Waddlesworth	6202	8/31/99	7	5	
Washington	6255	4/26/01	7	5	
Watson	6065	1996	5	25	
Weatherby	6283	10/1/01	7	5	
Wee Willie	6021	1995	4, 5	70, 5	w/overalls
Wee Willie	6021	1995	2, 4	65, 75	w/overalls & ribbon
Wee Willie	6021	1995	2, 5	30, 50	no clothes w/ ribbon
Wee Willie	6021	1995	2	65	w/overalls w/Wee Wiljje tag
Wee Willie	6021	1995	2	50	no clothes w/ Wee Wiljje tag
Whiskers	6012	1994	6, 7	5, 5	w/jumper
Whiskers	6012	1994	1, 5	85, 6	w/ribbon, w/overalls
William	6113	4/12/99	7	6	
Winifred	6302	4/30/02	7	5	
Winona	6300	4/30/02	7	5	
Woolie Brown	6012	1993	1	500+ very rare	
Woolie Gold	6011	1993	1	500	

Baby Ty

Back Row: Baby Dangles, Baby Growlers, Baby's First Bear
Front Row: My Baby Horsey, Huggypup

These soft and plush characters are safe for babies and in 1999 replaced Pillow Pals, the first baby collection introduced in 1995. Some of the 2001 and 2002 Baby Ty characters have "The Pillow Pals Collection" hang tags. Dolls and animals often come in a variety of colors, usually including pink and blue. The fabric "melts in your hands," making them the perfect toy for baby to cuddle.

Baby Petals

Baby Pups

Name	Style	Intro	Gen	$	Note
Baby Blooms	34602	12/30/04	2	10	blue
Baby Blossoms	34600	12/30/04	2	9	yellow petals
Baby Blue Bear	31015	10/31/06	2	8	blue
Baby Dangles	31024	10/31/06	2	8	blue
Baby Dangles	31023	10/31/06	2	8	pink
Baby Growlers	31032	12/29/06	2	8	blue
Baby Growlers	31031	12/29/06	2	8	pink
Baby Petals	34601	12/30/04	2	15	pink petals
Baby Pink	31014	10/31/06	2	8	pink
Baby Pups	31034	2/28/07	2	8	blue
Baby Pups	31033	2/28/07	2	8	pink
Baby Tiptop	31030	12/29/06	2	8	blue
Baby Tiptop	31029	12/29/06	2	8	pink

Baby Tiptop

Blessings to Baby

Name	Style	Intro	Gen	$	Note
Baby Whiffer	31026	10/31/06	2	8	blue
Baby Whiffer	31025	10/31/06	2	8	pink
Baby Winks	31028	10/31/06	2	8	blue
Baby Winks	31027	10/31/06	2	8	pink
Baby's First Bear	31042	10/31/07	2	8	blue
Baby's First Bear	31041	10/31/07	2	8	pink
Bearbaby	3209	1/1/00	1	15	blue
Bearbaby	3210	1/1/00	1	15	pink
Bearbaby	3200	1/1/01	1	20	ty dye
Blessings to Baby	34508	1/31/05	2	12	blue
Blessings to Baby	34510	1/31/05	2	12	green
Blessings to Baby	34511	1/31/05	2	12	pink
Blessings to Baby	34507	1/31/05	2	12	white
Blessings to Baby	34509	1/31/05	2	12	yellow

Cuddle Bunny

Cuddlekitty

Name	Style	Intro	Gen	$	Note
Bunnybaby	3204	1/2000	1	18	green
Bunny Hop	34513	1/1/06	2	8	blue
Bunny Hop	34512	1/1/06	2	9	pink
Cubby Cuddles	31010	7/29/05	2	8	pink
Cuddle Bunny	34501	12/30/04	2	16	blue
Cuddle Bunny	34502	12/30/04	2	16	pink
Cuddlecub	3301	11/1/01	1	18	blue
Cuddlecub	3300	11/1/01	1	18	pink
Cuddlekitty	32005	10/20/04	2	22	pale yellow
Cuddlepup	3303	11/1/01	1	45	green
Cuddlepup	34001	6/30/04	2	22	yellow blanket
Cuddleteddy	34100	6/30/04	2	20	blue blanket
Cutsiemoosie	3307	3/3/02	2	60	blue w/gold antlers
Dogbaby	3205	1/2000	1	14	yellow/pink

Funky Monkey

Gwowls

Name	Style	Intro	Gen	$	Note
Elephantbaby	3207	7/1/00	1	15	green/yellow
Elephanthugs	3310	4/30/02	2	60	pink
Frogbaby	3201	1/2000	1	40	green/yellow
Funky Monkey	31006	6/23/06	2	12	bright multi
Gwowls	31019	6/30/06	2	8	pink
Hippobaby	3206	7/2000	1	50	yellow/pink
Honeybunnybaby	3212	1/1/01	1	12	pale gold
Huggybunny	3305	12/28/01	1	30	blue
Huggybunny	3304	12/28/01	1	20	lilac pink
Huggyducky	3309	3/3/02	2	60	yellow
Huggypup	31008	10/29/04	2	8	tan
Kitty Cat	31004	6/30/05	2	10	bright multi
Kittybaby	3211	1/1/01	1	13	green
Kittyhugs	31009	10/29/04	2	7	cream

Little Piggy

My Baby Bear

Name	Style	Intro	Gen	$	Note
Kuddlekitty	3302	11/1/01	1	25	yellow
Kutie Kat	31012	7/29/05	2	7	lt. cream
Lamy	3202	1/1/00	1	30	gold/yellow
Little Piggy	31007	6/30/05	2	10	bright multi
Monkeybaby	3203	1/2000	1	35	lavender/pink
Moocowbaby	3208	7/2000	1	10	green/pink
My Baby Bear	34503	1/31/05	2	8	tan
My Baby Bear	31021	9/29/06	2	13	white, Christmas
My Baby Bear	34515	1/1/06	2	8	blue
My Baby Bear	34514	1/1/06	2	8	pink
My Baby Bunny	34505	1/31/05	2	8	white
My Baby Horsey	31036	6/29/07	2	8	blue
My Baby Horsey	31035	6/29/07	2	8	pink
My Christmas Bear	31038	9/28/07	2	8	white

PJ Bear

P'nut

Name	Style	Intro	Gen	$	Note
My Little Angel	31037	9/28/07	2	8	white
Peekiepoo	3311	4/30/02	1	26	green/pink
PJ Bear	31200	6/30/04	1	22	large blue
PJ Bear	31202	6/30/04	1	15	large green
PJ Bear	31203	6/30/04	1	22	large pink
PJ Bear	31201	6/30/04	1	15	large yellow
PJ Bear	31101	6/30/04	1	10	medium blue
PJ Bear	31103	6/30/04	1	18	medium green
PJ Bear	31104	6/30/04	1	10	medium pink
PJ Bear	31102	6/30/04	1	18	medium yellow
PJ Bear	31000	6/30/04	1	8	small blue
PJ Bear	31002	6/30/04	1	12	small green
PJ Bear	31003	6/30/04	1	8	small pink
PJ Bear	31001	6/30/04	2	12	small yellow

Snugglepup

Twacks

Name	Style	Intro	Gen	$	Note
P'nut	31017	6/30/06	2	8	yellow
Pretty Pony	34517	1/31/06	2	8	blue
Pretty Pony	34516	1/31/06	2	8	pink
Pretty Pony	31022	9/29/06	2	8	white
Pretty Puppy	31005	6/30/05	2	12	bright multi
Snooziepup	34002	6/30/04	2	20	green blanket
Snoozieteddy	34103	6/30/04	2	14	pink blanket
Snugger Pup	31011	7/29/05	2	8	blue
Snugglefrog	3306	12/28/01	1	22	green/pink
Snugglepup	32004	10/29/04	2	22	tan, green blanket
Twacks	31020	6/30/06	2	8	blue
Tygerhugs	3308	3/3/02	2	55	gold/black stripes

Ty Basket Beanies

Top Row: Eggs III, Hippity, Eggs II, Floppity, Eggs I
Bottom Row: Chickie, Ewey, Hippie

Basket Beanies are Ty's Easter series. Six were produced in spring 2002, and a new set each spring since. The 3" Basket Beanies are much smaller than Beanie Babies and have ribbon loops sewn to their tops so they can be hung as decorations. Some Beanies are smaller versions of the regular sized ones. The smaller tags say "Basket Beanies" on the front. All Basket Beanies have 1st Generation hang tags.

Baskets

Billingsly

Name	Style	Intro	$	Note
Baashful	35052	12/30/04	3	lamb
Baskets	35053	12/30/04	3	bunny
Billingsly	35072	12/30/05	3	duck
Bobsy	35087	1/31/07	4	bunny
Candies	35051	12/30/04	3	bear
Carnation	3537	1/30/04	3	cat
Chickie	3526	1/30/03	4	duck
Coop	35103	1/2/08	4	chick
Duckling	35054	12/30/04	3	chick in egg
Eggbert	3510	1/29/02	3	bear
Eggs I	3509	1/29/02	4	bear

Eggs III

Grace

Name	Style	Intro	$	Note
Eggs II	3524	1/30/03	3	bear
Eggs III	3525	1/30/03	3	lamb
Ewey	3512	1/29/02	3	bunny
Flipsy	35088	1/31/07	4	bunny
Floppity	3511	1/29/02	3	bunny
Floxy	35104	1/2/08	4	lamb
Grace	3513	1/29/02	3	bunny
Hippie	3527	1/30/03	3	bunny
Hippity	3514	1/29/02	3	bunny
Hobsy	35087	1/31/07	4	bunny

Mipsy

Nibbles

Name	Style	Intro	$	Note
Hopson	35105	1/2/08	4	bunny
Lullaby	3540	1/30/04	3	bunny
Marshmallow	35073	12/30/05	3	lamb
Meekins	35075	12/30/05	3	lamb
Mipsy	35088	1/31/07	4	bunny
Nibbles	3539	1/30/04	3	bunny
Petey	3538	1/30/04	3	bunny
Pipsy	35088	1/31/07	4	bunny
Sugartwist	35074	12/30/05	3	bunny
Topsy	35087	1/31/07	4	bunny

Top Row: Decade, Clubby VI
Bottom Row: SCARED-e, Chickie, Dizzy, Hamlet

Ty Beanie Babies

Ty created the "Original Nine" Beanie Babies in 1993 and began releasing them in early 1994. There are now more than twenty different collections, but Beanie Babies are still the most popular and largest collection. They are made from a variety of fabrics, are stuffed lightly, and are weighted with pellets. The soft toys are cuddly and poseable. Each Beanie has its own name and most of them have a birth date and poem included on the tag.

#1 Teacher

123's

Name	Style	Bday	Gen	$	Note
#1 Bear	none	none	5	5,500	
#1 Teacher	44054	5/3/05	13	7	Ty Store
123's	40655	8/22/06	15	7	
1997 Holiday Teddy Bear	4200	12/25/96	4	12	
1998 Holiday Teddy Bear	4204	12/25/98	5	12	
1999 Holiday Teddy Bear	4257	12/25/99	5	9	
1999 Signature Bear	4228	none	5	7	
2000 Holiday Teddy	4332	12/24/00	6, 7	7, 7	
2000 Signature Bear	4266	none	6, 7	7, 10	
2001 Holiday Teddy	4395	12/24/00	7, 9	7, 7	
2001 Signature Bear	4375	none	7, 9	7, 7	
2002 Holiday Teddy	4564	12/20/01	7, 10	10, 7	

2001 Signature Bear

2003 Holiday Teddy

Name	Style	Bday	Gen	$	Note
2002 Signature Bear	4565	none	7, 10	10, 7	
2003 Holiday Teddy	40028	12/25/03	7, 11	7, 7	
2003 Signature Bear	40011	none	7, 11	7, 7	
2004 Holiday Teddy	40139	12/25/04	12	7	
2004 Signature Bear	40158	none	12	7	
2005 Holiday Teddy	40274	12/24/04	13	7	
2005 Signature Bear	40285	none	13	7	
2006 (New Year)	44064	1/1/06	13	12	Ty Store
2006 Holiday Teddy	40443	12/25/06	14	7	
2006 Signature Bear	40458	none	14	7	
2006 Zodiac Dog	46051	1/29/06	13	7	
2007 (New Year)	44096	1/1/07	14	25	Ty Store

2005
Holiday
Teddy

2005 Signature
Bear

2007 Holiday Teddy

4-H

Name	Style	Bday	Gen	$	Note
2007 Holiday Teddy	44096	1/1/07	15	7	red, green
2007 Signature Bear	40721	none	15	7	
2007 Zodiac Pig	46088	2/18/07	14	20	Asian-Pacific
2008 (New Year)	44122	1/1/08	15	12	Ty Store
2008 Zodiac Rat	none	2/7/07	special	20	Asian-Pacific
4-H	40278	10/2/04	13	12	
A (alphabet bear)	40501	none	special	4	
ABC's	40655	8/22/06	15	7	
Aces	40380	1/8/06	14	7, 25*	*Knott's Berry Farm
Addison	4362	5/20/01	8	7, 40*	*Chicago Cubs game
Admiral	40392	12/28/05	14	7, 15*	*Santa Barbara Zoo
Adonis	48409	2/1/05	special	10	BBOM: 2/05

Aces

Name	Style	Bday	Gen	$	Note
Adore	44043	2/14/05	13	7	
Ai	4628	2/11/03	11	20, 150	Japan, Ty Store Japan
Alabama	40318	none	15	7, 7*	Trade Show, *Ty Store
Alana	40368	3/27/06	14	7	
Alani	48402	7/1/04	special	7	BBOM: 6/04
Alberta Wild Rose	46035	none	13	20	Trade Show
Allegro	40341	7/14/05	14	7	
All-Star Dad	40359	6/18/06	14	8	
Ally	4032	3/14/94	1, 2	1,800, 325	
Ally	4032	3/14/94	3, 4	50, 12	
Almond	4246	4/14/99	5	7	
Alpha Key-clip	46063	none	14	7	small

Addison

Alana

Allegro

All-Star Dad

Ally

Name	Style	Bday	Gen	$	Note
Alps	48404	9/1/04	special	8	BBOM: 9/04
Always	40161	2/14/04	12	7, 130*	*Convention
Amber	4243	2/21/99	5	7	
America (blue)	4506	none	7	7, 40*	*with Japanese writing
America (red)	4412	none	10	10, 175*	*Ty Store reversed ears
America (white)	4409	none	10	7, 7	Ty Store, 1 w/ reversed ears
American	40624	6/14/06	15	7	
American Blessing	40238	12/2/04	13	7, 20*	Knott's Berry Farm
Amigo	4422	8/3/03	11	10	Ty Store
Anchor	40395	3/22/06	14	7	
Ants	4195	11/7/97	5	7	
Aotearoa	46044	5/23/05	13	20, 675	Asian-Pacific, New Zealand

Amber

American

Amigo

Ants

April

April Fool

Aria

Arlene

Aruba

Name	Style	Bday	Gen	$	Note
April	4391	none	10	7	potbelly
April 2003	4555	none	special	7	new face
April Fool	44102	4/1/07	15	7	Ty Store
Arabesque	40339	9/13/05	14	7	
Aria	40092	7/30/03	12	7	
Ariel	4288	none	6, 7	7, 7	
Arizona	40300	none	13	7	sold only in Arizona
Arlene	40110	none	12	9	Garfield
Aruba	4314	4/8/00	6, 7	7, 7	
Astra	48406	11/1/04	special	15	BBOM: 11/04
Atlanta	40090	12/29/03	12	7	Trade Show
August	4371	none	14	7	potbelly

August

Austin

Avalanche

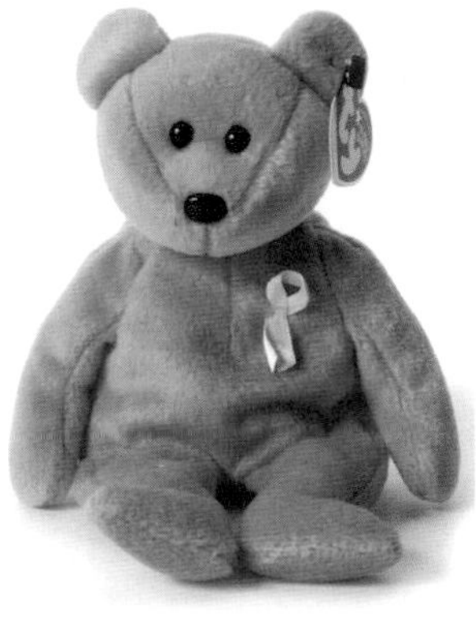

Aware

B.B. Bear

Name	Style	Bday	Gen	$	Note
August 2002	4547	none	14	7	new face
Aurora	4271	2/3/00	6, 7	7, 7	
Aussiebear	4626	1/25/03	11	20	Australia
Austin	40404	none	14	7	Backyardigans
Australia	46025	1/12/05	13	20	Australia
Avalanche	40689	3/18/07	15	7	
Avalon	40095	2/5/04	12	7	gold "Ty" tush tag
Aware	40271	10/10/04	13	7	
Awareness	40422	10/27/06	14	7	
B (alphabet bear)	40502	none	special	4	
B.B. Bear	4253	none	5	7	
Baaabsy	40376	4/7/06	14	7	

Baby Boy

Baby Girl

Name	Style	Bday	Gen	$	Note
Baaabsy Bag	40448	none	15	7	
Baby Boy	4534	3/3/02	7, 10	7, 7	
Baby Boy	40223	none	13	7	holding baseball
Baby Boy	40424	none	14	7	with night cap
Baby Girl	4535	1/19/02	7, 10	7, 10	
Baby Girl	40222	none	13	7	holding blanket
Baby Girl	40425	none	14	7	with night cap
Baby Jaguar	40571	none	15	7	Japan: Go Diego Go
Badges	40177	12/1/04	13	7	
Bahati	44024	none	12	7	Ty Store: World Wildlife Fund
Baldy	4074	2/17/96	4, 5	10, 7	
Bali	40187	8/8/04	13	7	grey

Bahati

Baldy

Bam

Bananas

Bandito

Name	Style	Bday	Gen	$	Note
Bali	40385	8/8/04	14	9	USA (blue)
Bali	47029	8/8/04	14	25	Shedd Aquarium
Bali Key-clip	47030	none	14	20	Pizza Hut
Bam	4544	11/25/01	7, 10	7, 7	
Bananas	4316	6/30/00	6, 7	7, 7	
Bandage	40221	12/3/04	13	7	
Bandito	4543	11/2/01	7, 10	7, 7	
Banjo	40085	10/1/03	12	7	gold "Ty" tush tag
Barbaro	40464	4/29/03	14	7, 30*	*Kentucky Derby
Barklowe	48428	9/1/06	special	12	BBOM: 9/06
Barley	40613	9/25/06	15	7	
Baron Van Pyre	40575	10/20/06	15	7	
Basilico	46062	6/9/06	14	20	UK
BAT-e	4429	10/31/03	11	10	
Batty	4035	10/29/96	5	7	ty-dye body

Barbaro

Baron Van Pyre

Batty

Beani

Bearon

Beary Bag

Bernie

Berry Ice

Name	Style	Bday	Gen	$	Note
Batty	4035	10/29/96	4, 5	7, 7	brown body
BayStars	46072	11/11/92	14	25	Japan
Beak	4211	2/3/98	5	7	
Beani	4397	7/26/00	7, 9	7, 7	
Bearon (brown)	40039	12/17/03	7, 11	20, 165*	*Midwest Airlines
Bearon (red)	40039	12/17/03	7, 11	12, 125*	*Midwest Airlines
Beary Bag	40489	none	15	7	
Beary Much	44100	none	15	7	
Benjamin	40239	1/17/1706	13	7	
Bernie	4109	10/3/96	4, 5	7, 7	
Berry Ice	40678	6/23/07	15	7	Trade Show
Bessie	4009	6/27/95	3, 4	55, 12	
Bianca	40156	9/15/04	12	7	

Bessie

Bidder

Name	Style	Bday	Gen	$	Note
Bidder	4980	9/24/03	12	36	Ty MBNA
Big Apple	40120	2/2/04	12	7	Trade Show
Bijoux	40104	7/21/04	12	7	
Billingham	48422	3/1/06	special	7	BBOM: 3/06
Billionaire Bear 1 & 2	none	none	5	750, 1,800	Ty Employee
Billionaire Bear 3 & 4	none	none	6, 9	900, 800	Ty Employee
Billionaire Bear 5	none	none	7, 10	875, 800	Ty Employee
Billionaire Bear 6	none	none	7, 11	700, 700*	Ty Employee
Billionaire Bear 7 & 8	none	none	12, 13	800, 800	Ty Employee
Billionaire Bear 9	none	none	14	800	Ty Employee
Binksy	40186	6/4/04	13	7	
Bits	49009	3/4/04	12	7, 16*	*in box
Bixby	40151	9/30/04	12	7	

Billingham

Binksy

Bixby

Blessed

Blackie

Blizzard

BLARN-e

Bloom

Name	Style	Bday	Gen	$	Note
Blackie	4011	7/15/94	1	3,000	
Blackie	4011	7/15/94	2, 3, 4, 5	300, 50, 10, 7	
BLARN-e	4436	3/17/04	12	10	Ty Store
Blessed	40010	10/11/02	7, 11	7, 7	
Bliss	40724	1/28/07	15	7	
Blissful	40628	none	15	7	
Blitz	40248	2/6/05	13	7	
Blizzard	4163	12/12/96	4, 5	7, 7	
Bloom	4596	4/29/03	7, 11	7, 7	
Bloom	4596	4/29/03	11	150	FTD Florida Convention
Bloomfield	40343	5/7/05	14	7	
Blue	4424	1/17/03	11	7	Ty Store
Blue	40344	none	14	7	Blues Clues
Blue	48324	none	14	7	USPS

Blue

Bo

Bones

Bongo

Bonzer

Name	Style	Bday	Gen	$	Note
Bluebonnet	40351	6/22/05	14	7	
Bo	4595	10/8/02	7, 11	7, 7	
Bodkin	40634	9/28/07	special	20	Boblins: Australia., Canada, New Zealand
Bones	4001	1/18/94	2, 3, 4, 5	235, 50, 7, 7	
Bones	4001	1/18/94	1st	2,500	
Bongo (tan tail)	4067	8/17/95	3, 4, 5	65, 7, 7	tan tail
Bongo (brown tail)	4067	8/17/95	3, 4	50/10	brown tail
Bonnet	44046	3/27/05	13	7, 20*	Ty Store, *Harrods UK
Bonsai	4567	11/5/01	7, 10	7, 7	
Bonzer	46110	8/1/07	15	20	Beales UK
Bonzer	40022	7/28/03	7, 11	12, 12	
Books	40266	8/15/04	13	9	(3) packs: red, blue, purple

Booties

Boots – Ice Skating

Bride

Brigitte

Name	Style	Bday	Gen	$	Note
Booties	4536	3/26/02	7, 10	7, 7	
Boots	40665	none	15	7	Dora the Explorer
Boots - Ice Skating	40693	none	15	7	Dora the Explorer
Boo Who?	47080	10/28/06	15	7	
Boston	40124	12/16/03	12	12	Trade Show
Bounder	46108	2/17/07	special	15	Australia
Bounds	40653	2/23/07	15	7	
Bravo Key-clip	46087	none	14	4	
Breadcrumbs	48412	5/1/05	special	7	May 2005 BBOM
Bride	4528	none	7, 10	7, 7	
Brigitte	4374	4/20/00	7, 9	10, 10	
Britannia	4601	12/15/97	5th	30	China w/ embroidered flag
Britannia	4601	12/15/97	5th	50	Indonesia w/ embroidered flag
Britannia	4601	12/15/97	5th	125	UK w/ patch flag

Britannia

Bronty

Brownie

Bubbles

Bubbly

Name	Style	Bday	Gen	$	Note
British Columbia Pacific Dogwood	46038	none	13	20*	Canadian Show
Bronty	4085	11/22/94	3	400	
Brownie	49030	none	special	125	BBOC Original 9, Set 3
Brownie	4010	none	1	2,800	
Bruno	4183	9/9/97	5	7	
Brutus	40482	9/9/06	15	7	
Bubbles	4078	7/2/95	3, 4	75, 35	
Bubbly	4985	2/16/03	11	7	Trade Show
Buckingham	4603	10/16/00	7	75	UK
Bucky	4016	6/8//1995	3,4	50, 7	
Bumble	4045	10/16/95	3, 4	250/325	
Bunga Raya	4615	2/1/02	10	20	Malaysia
Busby	40456	3/7/06	14	7	
Bushy	4285	1/27/00	6, 7	7, 7	

Bucky

Bushy

Buttercream

Buzzie

Name	Style	Bday	Gen	$	Note
Butch	4227	10/2/98	5	7	
Buttercream	4803	4/1/03	special	7	BBOM: 4/03
Buzzie	4354	10/20/00	7, 8	7, 7	
Buzzy	4308	7/6/00	6, 7	7, 7	
C (alphabet bear)	40503	none	special	7	
Cabaret	40415	7/19/06	14	7	
Caipora	44206	none	13	10	Ty Store: World Wildlife Fund
California	40083	none	12	7, 25*	*Knott's Berry Farm
California Poppy	40292	none	13	7, 25	Trade Show, Knott's Berry Farm
Canada	46017	none	12	15	Canada
Canada Key-clip	46075	none	14	8	Canada
CAND-e	4417	12/13/01	10	7	Ty Store

CAND-e

Canters

Name	Style	Bday	Gen	$	Note
Candy Canes	47082	12/19/06	15	7	Hallmark: red, white
Canters	48423	4/1/06	special	7	BBOM: 4/06
Canyon	4212	5/29/98	5	7	
Cappuccino	4804	5/1/03	special	7	BBOM: 5/03
Captain	40245	1/24/05	13	7	
Cargo	40685	12/19/06	15		(2) red, green
Carnation	4575	6/22/02	7, 11	7, 7	
Carrots	4512	9/13/01	7, 10	7, 7	
Casanova	40476	2/14/06	14	8	
Cashew	4292	4/22/00	6, 7	7, 7	
Cassie	4340	7/12/00	7, 8	7, 7	
Catsby	40361	7/24/05	14	7	
Caw	4071	none	3	350	
Celebrate	4385	3/13/01	7, 9	7, 7	
Celebrations	4620	none	7, 10	20, 20	

Cappuccino

Carnation

Cashew

Cassie

Caw

Celebrations

Champion - USA

Name	Style	Bday	Gen	$	Note
Champion - USA	4408	none	7, 10	7, 7	FIFA: 30 countries w/same value

Argentina
Belgium
Brazil
Cameroon
China PR
Costa Rica
Croatia
Denmark
Ecuador
England
France
Germany
Republic of Ireland
Italy
Mexico
Nigeria
Paraguay
Poland
Portugal
Russia
Saudi Arabia
Senegal
Slovenia
South Africa
Spain
Sweden
Tunisia
Turkey
Uruguay
USA

ChariTee

Charmer

Cheddar

Cheeks

Name	Style	Bday	Gen	$	Note
Champion - Japan	4408	none	10	20	FIFA: w/ Japanese writing
Champion - Korea	4408	none	10	20	FIFA: w/ Korean writing
ChariTee	40080	3/25/04	12	9	USA
Charles	46085	11/4/06	14	25, 125*	Harrods UK, *boxed
Charlie	40403	4/23/06	14	7	
Charm	40349	9/27/05	14	7	
Charmer	4568	9/10/02	7, 10	7, 7	
Charming	40314	1/17/05	13	7	
Chaser	40654	1/11/07	15	7	
Cheddar	4525	3/24/02	7, 10	7, 7	tan or blue body
Cheek to Cheek	40472	10/21/06	14	7	
Cheeks	4250	5/18/99	5	7	

Chickie

Chillin'

Name	Style	Bday	Gen	$	Note
Cheery	4359	8/18/00	7, 8	7, 7	dark or light blue clouds
Cheesly	40240	11/15/04	13	7	
Cheezer	4301	5/9/00	6, 7	7, 7	
Chef Robuchon	47045	9/18/06	14	4,000	NY Four Seasons L'Atelier
Cherry Ice	40678	6/23/07	15	7	Trade Show
Chessie	40660	6/2/07	15	7	
Chicago	40089	8/12/03	12	7	Trade Show
Chickie	4509	9/20/01	7, 10	7, 7	
Chili	40088	12/12/03	12	7	
Chillin'	40025	1/12/03	11	7	
Chillingsly	40446	1/21/06	14	7	

China

Chipper

Name	Style	Bday	Gen	$	Note
Chilly	4012	2/22/94	1	2,800	
Chilly	4012	2/22/94	2, 3	1,000, 900	
Chilton	48432	1/1/07	special	7	BBOM: 1/07
China	4315	9/4/00	6, 7	7, 7	
Chinook	4604	1/25/96	6	25	Canada
Chip	4121	1/26/96	4, 5	7, 7	
Chipper	4259	4/21/99	5	7	
Chitraka	44207	none	13	10	Ty Store: World Wildlife Fund
Chocolate	4015	4/27/93	1	2,500	
Chocolate	4015	4/27/93	2, 3	300, 60	
Chocolate	4015	4/27/93	4, 5	7, 7	

Chocolate

Chocolate Chip

Chops

Chopstix

Chuckles

Name	Style	Bday	Gen	$	Note
Chocolate	49021	4/27/93	special	7	BBOC Original 9, Sets 1-5
Chocolate Chip	47042	6/11/06	14	18	Midwest Airlines
Chocolate Kiss	47091	2/23/07	15	7	Walgreen's/Hershey
Chompers	48403	8/1/04	special	8	BBOM: 8/04
Chops	4019	5/3/96	3, 4	75, 50	
Chopstix	40047	1/22/03	12	7	
Chuckles	40172	10/23/04	13	7	
Cinders	4295	4/30/00	6, 7	7, 7	
Cinta	46005	11/25/03	12	7	Malaysia
Class of 2004	40066	3/15/04	12	8	
Classy	4373	4/30/01	8	7	Ty Store: The People's Beanie
Claude	4083	9/3/96	4, 5	7, 7	
Clover	4503	3/17/01	7, 9	7, 7	

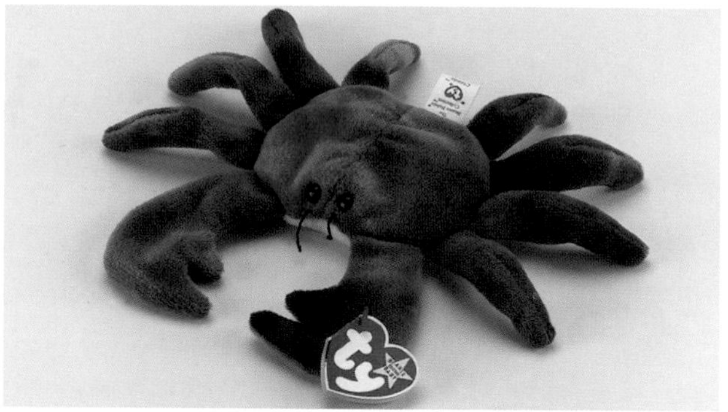

Claude

Clover

Clover (4-H Club Exclusive)

Clubby VIII

Clucky

Name	Style	Bday	Gen	$	Note
Clover	47012	10/2/04	13	12	4-H Club
Clubby	4991	7/7/98	5	10	BBOC
Clubby II	4992	3/9/99	5	8, 15*	BBOC, *Kit
Clubby III	4993	6/30/00	6, 7	10, 10	BBOC
Clubby IV	4996	8/4/01	9	20, 12, 7	Buttons: gold, silver, rainbow
Clubby V	4998	6/20/02	7, 10	10, 10	BBOC
Clubby VI	49000	4/9/03	7, 7, 11	12, 12, 12	blue, purple, rainbow
Clubby VII	49035	9/17/06	14	10	BBOC
Clubby VIII	04993	6/30/00	14	10	BBOC
Clucky	48427	8/1/06	special	7	BBOM: 8/06
Coastline	40630	8/7/06	15	7	
Coco Presley	47075	1/8/07	15	7	orange or brown
Cocoa Bean	47046	7/7/07	14	11	Walgreen's
Color Me Beanie	4989	12/11/01	7, 10	10, 10	bear

Coco Presley

Color Me Beanie B-day Kit - Dog

Name	Style	Bday	Gen	$	Note
Color Me Beanie	4988	7/24/02	7, 11	10, 10	bunny
Color Me Beanie B-day Kit	4901	none	10, 11	10, 10	cat
Color Me Beanie B-day Kit	4902	none	7, 11	10, 10	dog
Color Me Beanie B-day Kit	4903	none	7, 11	10, 10	bear
Color Me Beanie B-day Kit	4904	none	7, 11	10, 10	unicorn
Colorado	40123	none	12	7	sold only in Colorado
Colorado Columbine	40298	none	13	12	Trade Show
Colosso	40002	9/6/02	7, 11	7, 7	
Columbus	40134	3/3/03	12	10	Trade Show
Comet	4810	11/1/03	special	20	BBOM: 11/03
Congo	4160	11/9/96	4, 5	7, 7	
Cookies and Crème	47089	8/13/07	15	7	Walgren's/Hershey

Colosso

Congo

Cookies and Crème

Cool Chick

Coop

Name	Style	Bday	Gen	$	Note
Cool Cat	40215	none	15	7	Walgreen's
Cool Chick	40335	none	14	7	purse
Cool Clutch	40390	none	14	7	purse
Cool Teacher	40356	5/3/06	14	7	
Coolstina	40701	1/15/07	15	6	
Coolston	40702	1/15/07	15	6	
Coop	40493	7/12/06	15	7	
Copper	44118	9/18/07	15	7	Ty Store
Coral	4079	3/2/95	3, 4	100, 50	
Coral Casino	none	none	9	3,800	Coral Casino
Coreana	4629	10/3/02	11	20	Korea
Cornbread	4704	7/3/03	11	7	Cracker Barrel
Cornstalk	40614	11/10/06	15	7	
Corsage	40046	4/12/03	12	7	
Cottonball	4511	8/30/01	7, 10	7, 7	
Count	40116	9/8/03	12	7	

Coral

Cornbread

Cottonball

Countess

Croaks

Courage

Creepers

Name	Style	Bday	Gen	$	Note
Countdown	44027	1/1/05	12	10, 10, 35	Ty Store: 10/98, 7/6, 5/4, 3/2
Countess	48401	6/1/06	special	7	BBOM: 6/04
Courage	4515	none	9	7	flag on right/left leg, Japan
Courage	4515	none	9	8	flag on left or right leg
Courageous	46083	none	14	18	Canada
Courageously	46083	none	14	18	Canada
Courageousness	46083	none	14	18	Canada
Courageous	47043	none	14	150, 80	Special Olympics Canada, Festival
Courageously	47043	none	14	150, 80	Special Olympics Canada, Festival
Courageousness	46043	none	14	150, 80	Special Olympics Canada, Festival
Creepers	4376	10/18/00	7, 9	7, 7	

Cubbie

Cupid

Cupid's Bow

Cure

Curly

Name	Style	Bday	Gen	$	Note
Crinkles	40151	10/7/03	12	7	
Croaks	40178	12/8/04	13	7	
Crooner	40687	4/30/07	15	7	
Crunch	4130	1/13/96	4, 5	7, 7	
Cubbie	4010	11/14/93	1	3,000	
Cubbie	4010	11/14/93	2, 3	300, 60	
Cubbie	4010	11/14/93	4, 5	7, 7	
Cubbie	49029	11/14/93	special	10	BBOB Original 9: sets 1, 2, 4, 5
Cupid	4501	2/14/01	7, 9	7, 7	patch on left or right eye
Cupid's Bow	47094	2/13/07	15	7	Border's
Cure	40027	10/1/03	7, 11	7, 7	
Curls	40172	8/26/04	13	7	
Curly	4052	4/12/96	4, 5	7, 7	

Dad 2007

DAD-e 2003

Name	Style	Bday	Gen	$	Note
Curtsy	40627	11/11/06	15	7	
Cutesy	40149	4/10/04	12	7	
D (alphabet bear)	40504	none	special	4	
Dabbles	48424	5/1/06	special	7	BBOM: 5/06
Dad	40230	6/21/04	13	7, 7	holding letters
Dad 2006	44087	6/18/06	14	7	Ty Store
Dad 2007	44105	6/17/07	15	7	Ty Store
DAD-e	4413	6/16/02	10	20	Ty Store
DAD-e 2003	4421	6/15/03	11	10	Ty Store
DAD-e 2004	44012	6/20/04	12	9	Ty Store
Daffodil	4624	3/1/02	7	30	UK
Daichi	46090	4/19/06	15	20	Asian-Pacific
Dainty	40684	7/5/07	15	7	
Daisy	4006	5/10/94	1st	2,500	
Daisy	4006	5/10/94	2, 3	300, 50	
Daisy	4006	5/10/94	4, 5	7, 7	

Dainty

Daisy

Darling

Dart

Dear Dad

Dear Grandpa

Dearest

Dearly

Name	Style	Bday	Gen	$	Note
Daisy	4006	none	6	150	Harry Caray
Dancy	44113	7/27/07	15	7	Ty Store
Darling	4368	8/22/00	7, 9	7, 7	
Dart	4352	11/22/00	7, 8	7, 7	
Dear	4706	5/1/04	12	7	Hallmark
Dear Dad	47051	6/23/06	15	7	Hallmark
Dear Grandma	47050	5/9/06	15	9	Hallmark
Dear Grandpa	47052	6/26/06	15	7	Hallmark
Dear Heart	47024	5/12/05	14	10	Hallmark
Dear Mom	47049	5/27/07	15	7	Hallmark
Dear One	47023	5/8/05	14	10	Hallmark
Dearest	4350	5/8/00	7, 8	7, 7	
Dearly	47008	4/14/04	13	10	Hallmark
Decade	4585	1/22/03	11	10, 10	Ty Store

Decade

December

Name	Style	Bday	Gen	$	Note
Decade	4585	1/22/03	7, 11	10, 10	dark blue, orange, purple body
Decade	4585	1/22/03	7, 11	10, 10	green, gold body
Decade	4585	1/22/03	7, 11	10, 10	light blue, red, white body
Decade	4806	7/1/03	special	25	BBOM: 7/03, hot pink
December	4387	none	special	7	potbelly
December 2002	4551	none	special	7	new face
Deke	46054	1/26/04	14	15	Canada
Deke Key-clip	46077	none	14	7	Canada
Delights	44049	6/7/04	13	150	Ty Store: Pinky w/ Beanie tag
Delilah	40176	7/13/04	13	7	
Demure	40043	7/11/03	12	7	
Denver	40135	11/7/03	12	35	Trade Show
Deputy	40626	2/6/07	15	7	
Derby	4008	none	3	900	fine mane w/ no star

December 2002

Demure

Deputy

Derby

Deuce

Name	Style	Bday	Gen	$	Note
Derby	4008	9/16/95	3, 4, 5	125, 10, 10	coarse mane w/ no star
Derby	4008	9/16/95	5	7	coarse mane w/ star
Derby	4008	9/16/95	5	7	fur mane w/ star
Derby 132	40374	5/6/06	14	10, 25	USA, Kentucky Derby
Derby 133	40479	5/5/07	15	7, 20	USA, Kentucky Derby
Deuce	40417	8/28/06	14	7	USA
Deuce	47034	8/28/06	14	45	US Open
Deutschland	40091	5/9/03	12	9	
Deutschland	4639	5/9/03	12	22	German w/flag nose
Diddley	4383	7/25/00	7, 9	7, 7	
Diego	40423	none	14	7	Ty Store
Digger	4027	none	1	2,500	orange body
Digger	4027	none	2, 3	650, 350	orange body
Digger	4027	8/23/95	3, 4	150, 35	red body

Diddley

Digger

Diggs

Dinky

Dippy

Divalectable

Dizz

Dizzy

Name	Style	Bday	Gen	$	Note
Diggidy	40652	3/18/07	15	7	
Diggs	40142	10/17/03	12	7	
Dimples	44061	7/10/05	13	7	
Dinky	4341	9/25/00	7, 8	7, 7	
Dippy	4583	4/24/02	11	7	yellow, pink, or blue tummy
Discover	46007	6/20/04	12	50	Canada Show
Discover	47035	7/22/06	14	30	Northwestern Mutual: blue or gold
Divalectable	40409	7/7/06	14	7	
Divalectable Key-clip	40670	none	15	4	
Divalightful	40410	11/6/05	14	7	
Dizz	40585	8/26/07	15	7	
Dizzy	4365	10/7/00	8	125	Canada: black spots, ears, tail
Dizzy	4365	10/7/00	7	30	UK: colored ears, black spots

Doby

DOG

Doodle

Doogie

Dora – the Explorer

Name	Style	Bday	Gen	$	Note
Dizzy	4365	10/7/00	7, 8	9, 8	black ears w/ black spots
Dizzy	4365	10/7/00	7, 8	8 ,7	black ears w/ colored spots
Dizzy	4365	10/7/00	7, 8	8, 9	colored ears w/ colored spots
Dizzy Key-clip	40401	none	14	4	
Doby	4110	10/9/96	4, 5	7, 7	
Docks	40552	9/12/06	15	7	
Docks Key-clip	40559	none	15	4	
DOG	4326	none	6	9	Zodiac
Dominion	44016	7/1/04	12	15	
Donkey	47085	11/13/07	special	5	WalMart: mini in Shrek DVD
Doodle	4171	3/8/96	4	15	
Doogie	40362	8/12/05	14	7	
Dooley	40387	6/1/06	14	7	
Dora - the Explorer	40327	none	14	7	Ty Store
Dora - Cat Costume	40594	8/31/07	15	7	

Dora - Holiday

Dora - Mermaid

Name	Style	Bday	Gen	$	Note
Dora - China	40451	10/31/06	14	7	Ty Store
Dora - Del Tenis	40393	6/30/06	14	7	Ty Store
Dora - Del Tenis	47039	7/31/06	14	10	US Open
Dora - France	40454	10/31/06	14	7	Ty Store
Dora - Holiday	40445	9/29/06	14	8	
Dora - Ice Skating	40692	9/28/07	15	7	
Dora - Mermaid	40720	11/30/07	15	7	
Dora - Russia	40453	10/31/06	14	7	Ty Store
Dora - Tanzania	40452	10/31/06	14	7	Ty Store
Dora- Back to School	40622	7/31/07	15	7	
Dotson	40153	9/2/04	12	20	
Dotty	4100	10/17/96	4, 5	7, 7	
Down Under	46093	11/8/06	15	20	Asian-Pacific: Australian map
DRAGON	4322	none	6	9	Zodiac

Dotty

DRAGON

Dreamer

DUCK-e

Durango

Name	Style	Bday	Gen	$	Note
Dreamer	4802	3/1/03	special	14	BBOM: 3/03
Drumstick	44026	11/25/04	12	10	Ty Store
Dublin	4576	3/16/02	7, 11	7, 7	
DUCK-e	4425	6/21/02	11	10	Ty Store
Dundee	40190	9/19/04	13	12	
Durango	40087	6/3/04	12	7	gold "Ty" tush tag
Dusty	4702	5/4/03	11	125, 200	Chicago Cubs, with card
E (alphabet bear)	40505	none	special	4	
Early	4190	3/20/97	5	7	
Ears	4018	4/18/95	3, 4, 5	50, 7, 7	
Ebony	46121	2/7/07	15	20	Hamleys
Echo	4180	12/21/96	4, 5	8, 7	
Echo	4180	12/21/96	4	10	"Waves" tush tag
Eggbeart	4437	4/11/04	12	10	Ty Store

Early

Ears

Echo

Eggbert

Eggs

Eggs 2006

Name	Style	Bday	Gen	$	Note
Eggbert	4232	4/10/98	5	7	
Eggerton	40048	3/30/03	12	10	
Eggnog	44097	12/25/06	14	8	Ty Store
Eggs	4337	4/23/00	7, 8	8, 7	
Eggs 2004	40052	4/6/03	12	7	
Eggs 2005	40184	3/31/004	13	7	
Eggs 2006	40323	4/16/06	14	7	
Eggs 2007	40496	4/8/07	15	7	
Eggs II	4510	8/15/01	7, 10	7, 7	
Eggs III	4581	4/2/02	7, 11	7, 7	
Elfis	47058	3/13/06	14	10	Learning Express
Employee Bear	none	none	2	3,000	Ty Employee
Enchanting	40315	8/6/05	13	7	
Energizer Bunny	47087	11/23/07	15	7	Walgreen's

Eggs II

Eggs III

Energizer Bunny

Erin

Eucalyptus

Name	Style	Bday	Gen	$	Note
England	4608	10/5/01	7	20	England
England	46014	6/25/04	12	20	UK
Enigma	46096	6/15/06	15	30	Loch Ness Shop
Erin	4186	3/17/97	5	7	
Erin Key-clip	40334	none	14	6	
Eucalyptus	4240	4/28/99	5	7	
Ewey	4219	3/1/98	5	7	frowning or smiling
F (alphabet bear)	40506	none		4	
Fairydust	40357	3/24/06	14	7	
Fairytale	40189	11/22/04	13	7	
Fancy	40003	12/4/02	7, 11	7, 7	
Farley	40460	2/15/06	14	7	
Fauna	40648	5/19/07	15	7	
Fearless	46050	10/24/04	13	15	UK

Ewey

Fairytale

Fancy

Fauna

February

February 2003

Name	Style	Bday	Gen	$	Note
Feastings	48442	none	special	7	BBOM: 11/07
February	4389	none	10	7	2001 w/ potbelly
February 2003	4553	none	special	7	2002 w/ new face
Feder-bear	40480	8/8/81	14	7	Ty Store, Unicef for ACE
Feder-bear	40480	8/8/81	14	7	
Ferny	4618	2/6/02	10	20	New Zealand
Fetch	4189	2/4/97	5	7	
Fetcher	4289	4/27/00	6, 7	7, 7	
Fiddler	48408	1/1/05	special	12	BBOM: 1/05
Fidget	40005	1/20/03	7, 11	7, 7	
Filly	4592	7/16/02	7, 11	7, 7	
Finn	40394	5/14/06	14	7, 10	Ty Store, Sea Center
Fins	40033	3/4/03	7, 11	7, 7	

Feder-bear

Filly

Finn

Fireplug

Fizz

Name	Style	Bday	Gen	$	Note
Fireplug	48405	10/1/04	special	7	BBOM: 10/04
Fireworks	43438	7/1/07	special	10	BBOM: 7/07
First Dog	44088	7/4/06	14	7	Ty Store
Fitz	40097	1/10/04	12	7	gold "Ty" tush tag
Fizz	4983	2/16/03	11	8	Trade Show
Fizzer	40683	11/11/06	15	7	
Flaky	4572	1/31/02	7, 10	7, 7	
Flash	4021	5/13/93	1, 2	2,500, 300	
Flash	4021	5/13/93	3, 4	75, 35	
Flash	49019	5/13/93	special	10	BBOC: Orignial 9, sets 1-5
Flashy	4339	12/30/00	7, 8	7, 7	
Fleece	4125	3/21/96	4,5	7, 7	
Fleecie	4279	1/26/00	6, 7	7, 7	

Flash

Flashy

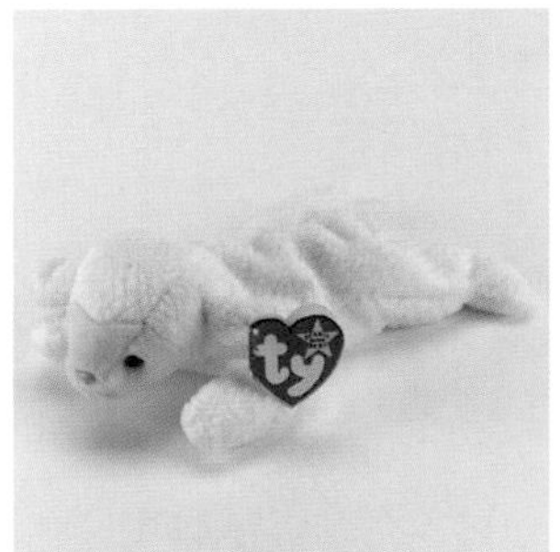

Fleece

Fleecie

Flitter

Float

Floppity

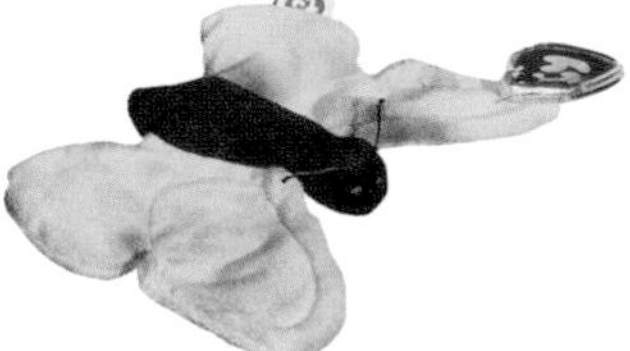

Flutter

Football Star

Fortune

Name	Style	Bday	Gen	$	Note
Fleur	40143	5/28/04	12	7	
Flicker	48419	12/1/05	special	7	BBOM: 12/05
Flip	4012	2/28/95	3, 4	60, 10	
Flitter	4255	6/2/99	5	7	
Float	4343	11/12/00	7, 8	7, 7	
Floppity	4118	5/28/96	4, 5	7, 7	
Flora	40647	3/9/07	15	7	
Florida	40147	none	12	7	sold only in Florida
Floxy	40498	1/11/07	15	7	
Fluff	40236	11/20/05	14	7	
Flurry	47015	12/2/05	13	7	
Flutter	4043	none	3	400	
Football Star	40463	none	14	7	
Forever Friends	40530	none	14	7	
Fortress	40650	5/22/07	15	7	

Frankenteddy

Free

Name	Style	Bday	Gen	$	Note
Fortune	4196	12/6/97	5	7	
Founders	48414	7/1/05	special	7	BBOM: 7/05
Fraidy	4379	10/13/00	7, 9	7, 7	
Frankenteddy	4562	10/31/01	7,10	7	different colored feet
Freckles	4066	6/3/96	4, 5	7, 7	Also has birthday of 7/28/1996
Free	44052	7/4/05	13	10	Ty Store: blue/silver star body
Free	40237	6/20/04	13	10	black body
Freezie	40439	12/20/05	14	7	
Freiherr von Schwarz	4611	6/17/01	7	35	German
Fridge	4579	11/10/02	7, 11	7, 75*	*Brookfield Zoo
Friedrich	46033	12/1/04	13	20	European
Friends	44109	none	15	9	Ty Store
Frightful	47031	9/1/06	14	7	Borders/Walden
Frigid	4270	1/23/00	6, 7	7, 7	

Friends

Frills

Frisbee

Frisco

Frolic

Frosty

Fun

Fuzz

Name	Style	Bday	Gen	$	Note
Frills	4367	3/5/01	7, 8	7, 7	
Frisbee	4508	6/29/01	7, 10	7, 7	
Frisbee	4508	6/29/01	10	150	Wham-O hang tag
Frisco	4586	9/7/02	7, 11	7, 7	
Frisky	48416	9/1/05	special	10	BBOM: 9/05
Fritters	48410	3/1/05	special	7	BBOM: 3/05
Frolic	4519	6/28/01	7, 10	7, 7	
Frosty	40009	12/7/03	7, 11	7, 7	
Fuddle	40625	2/25/07	15	7	
Fumbles	40171	9/1/04	13	7	
Fun	40383	2/12/06	14	10	20th Anniversary
Fun Key-clip	none	none	14	25	New York & Dallas Shows
Funky	40413	1/30/06	14	7	

Garcia

Garfield 4-H

Name	Style	Bday	Gen	$	Note
Furston	40434	11/18/05	14	7	
Fussy	40086	2/15/04	12	7	gold "Ty" tush tag
Fuzz	4237	7/23/98	5	7	
G (alphabet bear)	40507	none	special	4	
Garcia	4051	8/1/95	3, 4	175, 80	
Garfield	40114	none	12	8	Ty Store
Garfield with DVD	none	none	15	15	mini Garfield with DVD
Garfield 4-H	47037	none	14	15	4-H Club
Garfield Cool Cat	40215	none	13	8	Ty Store
Garfield Goodnight	40316	none	13	8	
Garfield Happy Holidays	40305	none	13	8	
Garfield Happy Valentines Day	40317	none	13	8	
Garfield His Majesty	40397	none	14	8	

Garfield
His Magesty

Garfield Love is ...

Gary the Snail

Georgia

Name	Style	Bday	Gen	$	Note
Garfield - I don't do perky	40668	none	15	8	
Garfield Key-clip	40603	none	15	4	
Garfield Love is ...	40727	none	15	7	
Garfield - Perfectly Lovable!	40629	none	15	8	Ty Store
Garfield Season's Greetings	40447	none	14	8	
Garfield - Stuck On You!	40487	none	14	8	Ty Store
Garlands	40706	12/19/06	15	7	
Gary the Snail	40469	none	14	7	SpongeBob
Gary the Snail Key-clip	47057	none	14	12	SpongeBob: Best Buy
George	46059	6/9/06	14	20	European

Germania

Ghoulish

Name	Style	Bday	Gen	$	Note
Georgia	40128	none	12	7	sold only in Georgia
Georgia Cherokee Rose	40291	none	13	10	Trade Show
Germania	4236	10/3/90	5	10, 50	English tag, German tag
Germany	46034	2/20/04	13	20	German
Ghostio	40579	10/25/06	15	7	
Ghoul	40260	11/1/04	13	7	
Ghoulianne	40260	11/1/04	13	7	
Ghoulish	40421	8/23/06	14	7	
Giblets	44060	11/24/05	13	10	Ty Store
Gift (Joy)	47003	11/7/03	12	10	Hallmark (green)
Gift (Love)	47005	11/7/03	12	10	Hallmark (white)

Gift

Giganto

GiGi

Giraffiti

Gizmo

Glacier

Name	Style	Bday	Gen	$	Note
Giganto	4384	12/17/00	7, 9	7, 7	
GiGi	4191	4/7/97	5	7	
Gimmy	40608	none	15	7	Boblins: Sweden/UK
Giraffiti	40060	8/31/03	12	7	
Giving	40572	10/25/07	15	7	
Giving Key-clip	40573		15	7	
Gizmo	4541	8/21/01	7, 10	7, 7	
Glacier	40714	5/17/07	15	7	
Glam Bag	40391	none	14	10	
Glider	4574	10/4/01	7, 10	7, 7	
Glory	4188	7/4/97	5	7	
Glow	4283	1/4/02	6, 7	7, 7	

Glider

Glory

Glow

GOAT

Gobbles

Goldie

Name	Style	Bday	Gen	$	Note
GOAT	4329	none	6	9	Zodiac
Goatee	4235	11/4/98	5	7	
Gobbles	4034	11/27/96	4, 5	7, 7	
Goddess	40054	5/27/03	12	7	
Goldie	4023	11/14/94	1, 2	1,800, 250	
Goldie	4023	11/14/94	3, 4, 5	60, 9, 7	
Goochy	4230	11/18/98	5	7, 7	light green or pink body
Goodheart	40686	10/20/07	15	7	
Goody	40275	9/6/05	13	8	
Gouliette	40579	9/29/06	15	7	
Grace	4274	2/10/00	6, 7	7, 7	
Gracie	4126	6/17/96	4, 5	7, 7	
Graf von Rot	4612	11/9/01	7	30	Germany

Goodheart

Goody

Grams

Grandfather

Gretel

Groom

Name	Style	Bday	Gen	$	Note
Gramps	44058	9/11/05	13	10	Ty Store
Grams	44057	9/11/05	13	10	Ty Store
Grandfather	44019	9/12/04	12	15	Ty Store
Grandmother	44018	9/12/04	12	15	Ty Store
Grape Ice	40678	6/23/07	15	7	Trade Show
Gratefully	40581	11/27/07	15	7	
Greetings	48407	12/1/04	special	7	BBOM: 12/04
Gretel	40703	1/10/07	15	7	
Grizzwald	40101	3/26/04	12	7	
Goody	40275	9/6/05	15	7	
Groom	4529	none	7, 10	7, 7	
Groovey	40412	7/22/06	14	7	
Groovy	4256	1/10/99	5	7	
Groowwl	40440	8/28/06	14	7	

Grumbles

Grunt

Groowwl

Hairy

Name	Style	Bday	Gen	$	Note
Grumbles	48425	6/1/06	special	7	BBOM: 6/06
Grunt	4092	7/19/95	3, 4	75, 40	
Gully	40608	none	15	7	Boblins: Canada/ Australia/N Zealand
Gussy	40450	none	14	7	Charlotte's Web
Gussy	47062	none	15	7	Charlotte's Web: Wal-Mart w/ DVD
Gypsy	40094	8/24/03	12	7	
H (alphabet bear)	40508	none	special	4	
Hairy	4336	10/6/00	7, 8	7, 7	
Halo	4208	8/31/98	5	7	
Halo II	4269	1/14/00	6, 7	7, 7	
Hamish	46082	11/30/06	14	16	UK flag

Halo

Halo II

Hamlet

Happy

Happy Birthday

Happy Hanukkah

Name	Style	Bday	Gen	$	Note
Hamlet	40016	11/13/02	7, 11	7, 7	
Hamley	46080	9/1/06	14	25	Hamley's UK
Hannah	46002	5/20/03	12	15	Japan
Hansel	40704	1/11/07	15	7	
Happily	47020	2/25/06	14	7	
Happy	4061	none	1	2,300	gray body
Happy	4061	none	2, 3	500, 300	gray body
Happy	4061	2/25/94	3, 4, 5	100, 7, 7	lavender body
Happy Birthday	40058	none	12	7	orange w/package
Happy Birthday	40198	none	13	7	red w/package
Happy Birthday	40234	none	13	7	smaller tan w/package
Happy Birthday	40224	none	13	7	yellow w/jester hat

Happy Holidays

Harry

Name	Style	Bday	Gen	$	Note
Happy Birthday	40259	none	13	7	orange w/jester hat
Happy Birthday	40328	none	14	7	tan w/party hat
Happy Birthday	40532	none	14	7	tan holding message
Happy Birthday	40483	none	15	7	tan w/cake on head
Happy Birthday	40617	none	15	7	blue w/party hat
Happy Birthday	40616	none	15	7	red w/party hat
Happy Hanukkah	40279	12/25/05	13	8, 8	with menorah or dreidel
Happy Holidays	47009	12/26/04	13	8	Hallmark Gold Crown
Happy Holidays	40537	none	14	8	bear holding message
Hark	40709	12/24/07	15	7	Cracker Barrel: red, green, white
Harrison	40194	5/2/04	13	7	
Harry	4546	12/9/01	7, 10	7, 7	
Haunt	4377	10/27/00	7, 9	7, 7	
Haunted	47071	10/28/06	15	7	

Haunt

Haunted

Heartthrob

Hearts-A-Flutter

Herald

Herder

Name	Style	Bday	Gen	$	Note
Haunting	40576	10/29/06	15	7	
Haunts	47032	9/1/06	14	7	
Harvester	40581	11/22/07	15	7	(3) green, red, white
Hawaii	40166	none	12	20	sold only in Hawaii
Hawthorne	40154	5/18/04	12	7	
Heartthrob	4813	2/1/04	special	7	BBOM: 2/04
Hearts-A-Plenty	47083	2/10/07	15	7	Hallmark
Hearts-A-Flutter	47083	2/10/07	15	7	Hallmark
Heavenly	40580	8/7/07	15	7	
Heiress	40079	4/20/04	12	7	gold "Ty" tush tag
Henry	46084	11/4/06	14	25, 90*	Harrods UK, *boxed
Herald	4570	1/7/02	7, 10	7, 7	

Hero

Hero 2003

Name	Style	Bday	Gen	$	Note
Herder	4525	8/29/01	7, 10	7, 7	
Hero (Dad)	4351	6/18/00	7, 8	7, 7	
Hero	40012	3/12/03	11,11	7,7	flag: left arm & reversed, chest
Hero	40012	3/12/03	11	150	Cody Banks movie premiere
Hero 2003	40013	3/12/03	11	7	UK flag
Hero 2003	40014	3/12/03	11	10	Ty Store, Australia flag
Hers	44013	none	12	7	Ty Store
Herschel	4700	4/26/02	10	7	Cracker Barrel
Hikari	46041	8/6/05	13	25	Asian-Pacific
Hikari	46049	8/6/05	13	60	Japan

Herschel

Hippie

Name	Style	Bday	Gen	$	Note
Hippie	4218	5/4/98	5	7	
Hippily	47020	2/25/06	14	7	Hallmark
Hippity	4119	6/1/96	4, 5	7, 7	
His	44014	none	12	7	Ty Store
Hissy	4185	4/4/97	5	7	
Ho Ho Ho	40538	none	14	7	
Hobo	40231	10/11/04	13	10	
Hocus	40262	10/29/04	13	7	
Hodge-Podge	4569	7/27/02	7, 10	7, 7	pink or blue front paws
Hodges	40651	5/17/07	15	7	
Holidays	44121	12/24/07	15	7	Ty Store

Hippity

Hissy

Hocus

Hodge-Podge

Hollydays

Holmes

Name	Style	Bday	Gen	$	Note
Hollydays	40273	12/15/04	14	7	
Hollyhorse	40444	12/4/05	14	7	
Holmes	4801	2/1/03	special	12	BBOM: 2/03
Holy Father	40265	none	13	7	gold "heart" on tush tag
Homeland	40364	6/14/06	14	7	
Honey-Bun	40159	6/25/04	12	7	white, pink or red
Honker	40719	10/26/07	5	7	
Honks	4258	3/11/99	5	7	
Honor Roll	44106	4/22/07	15	7	Ty Store
Honors	40358	5/31/06	14	7	
Hoodwink	40499	3/9/06	15	7	
Hoofer	4518	11/17/01	7, 10	7, 7	

Homeland

Honks

Honor Roll

Honors

Hoofer

Hoppington

Name	Style	Bday	Gen	$	Note
Hoops	40286	3/6/05	13	7	
Hoot	4073	8/9/95	3, 4	50, 10	
Hope	4213	3/23/98	5	7	
Hopper	4342	8/7/00	7, 8	7, 7	
Hoppily	47020	2/25/06	14	7	
Hoppington	47084	1/24/08	14	7	Hallmark
Hoppity	4117	4/3/96	4, 5	7, 7	
Hopson	40495	2/23/06	15	7	
Hornsly	4345	8/24/00	7, 8	7, 7	
HORSE	4324	none	6	9	Zodiac: pink or colored ears

Hornsly

Hopper

HORSE

Howl

Huggy

Name	Style	Bday	Gen	$	Note
Houston	40388	11/17/05	14	7	
Howl	4310	5/23/00	6, 7	9, 9	
Huggins	40077	10/18/03	12	7	
Huggy	4306	8/20/00	6, 7	7, 7	
Hug-hug	40310	2/15/05	13	7	
Hugsy	47047	7/7/07	14	7	Walgreen's, Hershey
Humphrey	4060	5/19/94	1	2,800	
Humphrey	4060	5/19/94	2, 3	1,000, 800	
Huntley	40107	7/16/03	12	7	
Hutch Clutch	40336	none	14	10	
I (alphabet bear)	40509	none	special	4	
I ♥ U	40307	2/19/05	13	10	
Icecubes	48420	1/1/06	special	20	BBOM: 1/06

Hug-hug

Huntley

I ♥ U

Iggy

Inch

India

Name	Style	Bday	Gen	$	Note
Icepack	44205	none	13	10	Ty Store: World Wildlife Fund
Icing	40241	12/18/04	13	7	
Iggy	4038	8/12/97	5	7	blue or tie dyed w/no tongue
Iggy	4038	8/12/97	5	7	neon or pastel w/ tongue
Illinois	40127	none	12	10	sold only in Illinois
Illinois Violet	40293	none	13	10	Trade Show
Inch	4044	9/3/95	3, 4	100, 75	felt antennas
Inch	4044	9/3/95	4, 5	7, 7	yarn antennas
Independence	40366	7/4/06	14	7	blue, red, or white feet/brims
India	4291	5/26/00	6, 7	7, 7	
Inky	4028	none	1, 2	3000, 1500	tan with no mouth
Inky	4028	none	2, 3	600, 400	tan with mouth

Issy

Name	Style	Bday	Gen	$	Note
Inky	4028	11/29/94	3, 4, 5	125, 7, 7	pink with mouth
Ireland	46019	12/17/04	13	20	UK
Issy	4404	none	6	225	4 Seasons:New York
Issy	4404	none	7, 9	50, 40	Alexandria
Issy	4404	none	7, 9	25, 25	Budapest
Issy	4404	none	7, 9	75, 75	Costa Rica
Issy	4404	none	7, 8, 9	175, 175, 175	Kuala Lumpur
Issy	4404	none	7, 9	50, 50	Miami
Issy	4404	none	7, 8	575, 575	Santa Barbara
Issy	4404	none	7, 8, 9	100, 100, 90	Vancouver
Issy	4404	none	7, 8	575, 575	Santa Barbara
Issy	4404	none	7, 8	7, 7	4 Seasons: 10 hotels w/same value

Amman
Beirut
Doha
Jackson Hole
Puerto Rico
Riyadh
Sao Paulo
Sharm El Sheikh
Terre Blanche
Whistler

Name	Style	Bday	Gen	$	Note
Issy	4404	none	7, 8, 9	7, 7, 7	4 Seasons: 43 hotels w/same value

Atlanta
Austin
Bali
Bangkok
Berlin
Beverly Hills
Boston
Cairo
Caracas
Chiang Mai
Chicago
Dallas
Hong Kong
Houston
Hualalai
Istanbul
Jakarta
Las Vegas
Lisbon
London
Los Angelas
Maldives
Maui
Mexico City
Milano
Nevis
Newport Beach
Palm Beach
Paris
Philadelphia
Prague
Punta Mita
San Diego
San Francisco
Scottsdale
Seattle
Shanghai
Singapore
Sydney
Taipei
Tokyo
Toronto
Washington, DC

Jabber

Jake

January 2003

Jemima Puddle-duck

Name	Style	Bday	Gen	$	Note
It's A Boy	40056	none	12	9	
It's A Girl	40055	none	12	9	
Ivory	46120	1/7/07	15, 13	25, 20	Hamley's
J (alphabet bear)	40510	none	special	4	
Jabber	4197	10/10/97	5	7	
Jack	40071	6/14/03	12	12, 8	UK: flag nose, black nose
Jake	4199	4/17/97	5	7	
Janglemouse	40437	11/28/05	14	7	
January	4388	none	10	7	potbelly
January 2003	4552	none	special	7	new face
Japan	46022	2/11/04	13	25	Japan
Jaz	40074	4/25/04	12	7	
Jemima Puddle-duck	46069	none	14	12	UK: Beatrix Potter

Jester

Name	Style	Bday	Gen	$	Note
Jersey	48012	1/1/04		7	BBOM: 1/04
Jester	4349	9/30/00	7, 8	7, 7	
Jimbo	40064	10/2/03	12	7	
Jinglemouse	40436	11/28/05	14	7	
Jinglepup	4394	12/3/00	9	7	red hat with white tail
Jinglepup	4394	12/3/00	7	15	UK green hat, green tail
Jinglepup	4394	12/3/00	9	7	USA green hat, white tail
Jinglepup	4394	12/3/00	9	10	Singapore white hat, green tail
Jinglepup	4394	12/3/00	9	10	Canada white hat, white tail
Jinxed	48441	10/28/07	15	7	

Jinglepup

Jinxed

Johnny

Jokester

Name	Style	Bday	Gen	$	Note
Jinxy	44022	10/31/04	12	15	Ty Store
Joaquim	46004	1/28/04	12	15	Asian-Pacific
John	40329	10/30/1735	13	10	
Johnny	47044	6/24/06	14	12	4-H Club
Jokester	44045	4/1/05	13	10	Ty Store
Jolly	4082	12/2/96	4, 5	7, 7	
Joy	40442	12/24/05	14	7	
Joyful	40442	12/24/05	14	7	
Joyous	40442	12/24/05	14	7	
Jubilant	47081	12/27/06	15	7	silver or gold wings/ noses
Juggles	40277	10/9/04	13	7	
July	4370	none	10	7	potbelly
July 2003	4558	none	special	7	new face

Jolly

Juggles

July

July 2003

June 2002

Kaleidoscope

Name	Style	Bday	Gen	$	Note
Jumpshot	40073	8/14/03	12	7, 140*	*Brookfield Zoo
June	4393	none	10	10	potbelly
June 2002	4557	none	special	10	new face
Juneau	40100	12/17/03	12	7	
Junglelove	40471	4/18/06	14	7	same style as Lovesick
Jurgen	46061	6/9/06	14	7	European
K (alphabet bear)	40511	none	special	4	
Kaleidoscope	4348	6/24/00	7, 8	7, 7	
Kanata	4621	10/14/02	10	15	Canada: 13 bears w/same value

Alberta
British Columbia
Manitoba
New Brunswick
Newfoundland
Northwest Territories
Nova Scotia
Nunavut
Ontario
Prince Edward's Island
Quebec
Saskatchewan
Yukon

Khufu

Kicks

Name	Style	Bday	Gen	$	Note
Kansas	40130	none	12	10	Sold only in Kansas
Kansas City	40118	6/3/04	12	25	Trade Show
Kansas Sunflower	40294	none	13	10	Trade Show
Kernow	46057	3/5/06	14	20	UK
Kernow Key-clip	46102	none	15	10	UK
Khufu	4807	8/1/03	special	8	BBOM: 8/03
Kia Ora	46095	3/29/06	15	20	Asian-Pacific
Kicks	4229	8/16/98	5	7	
Killarney	40042	3/17/03	12	7	
Kippy	4902	9/1/03	special	9	BBOM: 9/03
Kirby	4396	5/5/01	7, 9	7, 7	
Kissable	40470	2/4/06	14	7	
KISS-e	4419	2/14/02	11	9	Ty Store

Kippy

Kirby

Kissable

KISS-e

Kiss-kiss

Kissme

Name	Style	Bday	Gen	$	Note
Kisses	47048	7/7/07	14	7	Walgreens, Hershey
Kiss-kiss	40130	2/15/05	13	7	
Kissme	4504	2/7/01	7, 9	7, 7	
Kissy	40037	2/7/03	11	7	
Kiwi	4070	9/16/95	3, 4	75, 40	
Kiwiana	4627	5/1/03	11	20	New Zealand
KnOWLwdge	47066	6/19/06	15	10	Borders/Walden
Knuckles	4247	3/5/99	5	7	
Kookie	40061	7/15/03	12	7	
Kooky	4357	10/24/00	7, 8	9, 9	
Koowee	46009	9/24/03	12	15	Australia, New Zealand
Koowee Key-clip	46107	none	12	5	

Kiwi

Knuckles

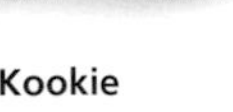

Kookie

Kooky

Kringle

KuKu

Name	Style	Bday	Gen	$	Note
Korea	46027	10/3/04	13	25	Korea, flag nose
Korea	46043	10/3/04	13	25	Asian-Pacific, black nose
Kringle	40138	12/24/04	12	7	
KuKu	4192	1/5/97	5	7	
L (alphabet bear)	40512	none	special	4	
LA	40117	4/4/04	12	7	Trade Show
Laguna	40646	6/26/06	15	7	
L'amore	40008	11/16/02	7, 11	7, 7	
Lani	40141	3/26/04	12	7	
Laptop	40150	8/9/04	12	7	
Las Vegas	40228	3/16/05	13	7	Las Vegas

L'amore

Laptop

Name	Style	Bday	Gen	$	Note
Laughter	40384	2/12/06	14	7	20th Anniversary
Laughter Key-clip	none	none	14	25	
Leaves	44092	9/23/06	14	25	Ty Store
Leelo	40661	7/18/06	15	7	
Leftovers	40574	11/23/07	15	7	
Lefty	4085	7/4/96	4	60	USA
Lefty 2000	4290	7/4/00	6	7	USA
Lefty 2004	40045	6/25/03	12	7	
Legend	40076	12/9/03	12	12	
Legs	4020	4/25/93	1, 2	1,400, 250	
Legs	4020	4/25/93	3, 4	60, 7	

Leaves

Leftovers

Lefty 2000

Legend

Legs

Leopold

Name	Style	Bday	Gen	$	Note
Legs	49018	4/25/93	special	10	BBOC: Original 9, sets 1-5
Lemonade Ice	40678	6/23/07	15	7	Trade Show
Leopold	47072	5/2/07	15	7	Rainforest Café
Lex	47001	9/10/04	12	12	Learning Express
Li Mei	44200	None	12	10	Ty Store
Libearty	4057	Summer1996	4	90	USA
LIBERT-e	44015	7/4/04	12	7	Ty Store
Liberty	4531	6/14/01	10	7, 7, 7	blue, red, or white face
Lightning	4537	3/27/02	7, 10	7, 7	
Lime Ice	40678	6/23/07	15	7	
Linah	44117	9/14/07	15	7	Ty Store

Libearty

Lightning

Lips

Little Feather

Little Squeeze

Lizzy

Name	Style	Bday	Gen	$	Note
Lips	4254	3/15/99	5	7	
Little Bear	40435	11/23/06	14	7	
Little Feather	40136	9/22/03	12	7	
Little Kiss	47040	2/7/06	14	7	Hallmark
Little Squeeze	47040	2/7/06	14	7	Hallmark
Little Star	47017	6/4/05	13	7	Little Star, Inc.
Lizzy	4033	none	3	400	tie-dye body
Lizzy	4033	5/11/95	3, 4, 5	100, 7, 7	blue body
Logger	40680	9/14/06	15	7	
Lollipup	40342	1/10/05	14	7	
London	46015	7/19/04	12	20	London
Loong	46045	9/9/05	13	20	Asian-Pacific

Loosy

Lot's O' Luck

Louisiana

Love U Mom

Name	Style	Bday	Gen	$	Note
Loosy	4206	3/29/98	5	7	
Lot's O' Luck	48434	3/1/07	special	7	BBOM: 3/07
Louis	40113	none	12	8	Garfield
Louisiana	40319	none	13	7	$1 to Red Cross
Louisiana	44078	none	13	7	Ty Store: $2 to Red Cross
Love and Kisses	40534	none	14	7	
Love Birds	47027	none	14	8	Hallmark Gold Crown
Love U Mom	40348	5/14/06	14	7	USA/Canada
Love U Mum	46056	3/26/06	14	7	UK/New Zealand/ Australia
Lovesick	40471	4/14/06	14	7	same style as Junglelove
Lovesme	44082	2/14/06	14	12	Ty Store

Lovey-Dovey

Lucky

LUCK-e

Luke

Name	Style	Bday	Gen	$	Note
Lovey-Dovey	40159	6/25/04	12	12	(3) pink, red, white
Loveypup	40725	3/2/07	15	7	
Luau	40069	8/21/03	12	12	
Luca	40111	none	12	8	Garfield
LUCK-e	4420	3/17/03	11	7	Ty Store
Lucky	4040	none	1	2,500	7 glued felt spots
Lucky	4040	none	2, 3	400, 150	7 glued felt spots
Lucky	4040	5/1/95	4, 5	7, 7	11 printed spots
Lucky	4040	5/1/95	4	125	21 printed spots
Lucky O' Day	40325	3/17/06	14	7	
Luke	4214	6/15/98	5	7	
Luke Key-clip	40402	None	14	4	
Lullaby	4583	5/17/02	7, 11	7, 7	

Lullaby

Lumberjack

Lurkey

M.C. Anniversary 3rd Edition

M.C. Anniversary 4th Edition

Name	Style	Bday	Gen	$	Note
Lumberjack	40001	3/22/03	7, 11	7, 7	
Lurkey	4309	6/13/00	6, 7	7, 7	
M (alphabet bear)	40513	None	special	4	
M.C. Anniversary 1st Edition	No style	2/10/02	11	100	Ty MBNA
M.C. Anniversary 2nd Edition	4982	8/10/03	11	100	Ty MBNA
M.C. Anniversary 3rd Edition	49009	7/29/04	12	100	Ty MBNA
M.C. Anniversary 4th Edition	49011	7/23/05	13	100	Ty MBNA
M.C. Anniversary 5th Edition	49032	10/24/06	14	100	Ty MBNA

M.C. Beanie III

M.C. Beanie VI

Name	Style	Bday	Gen	$	Note
M.C. Anniversary 6th Edition	49037	8/1/07	15, 13	100	
M.C. Beanie	4997	none	9	30	Ty MBNA, black or card nose
M.C. Beanie	4997	none	9	3,000	Ty MBNA, brown nose
M.C. Beanie II	4987	1/11/02	10	25	available w/ anniversary card.
M.C. Beanie III	4981	7/13/03	11	25	Ty MBNA
M.C. Beanie IV	49006	8/16/04	12	20	Ty MBNA
M.C. Beanie V	49010	8/5/05	13	15	
M.C. Beanie VI	49033	8/14/06	14	15	
M.C. Beanie VII	49036	8/17/07	15	7	
M.C. Beanie Key Clip	CC010	none	14	10	
Mac	4225	6/10/98	5	7	
Magenta	40346	none	14	7	Blues Clues

Mac

Magenta

Magic

Manchu

Mandy

Manes

Name	Style	Bday	Gen	$	Note
Magenta	48325	none	14	7	USPS
Magic	4088	9/5/95	4	75	hot pink thread
Magic	4088	9/5/95	3	75	pale pink thread
Magic	4088	9/5/95	4	7	medium pink thread
Majestic	46058	4/21/06	14	15	UK, Australia, New Zealand
Maju	46040	8/9/05	13	20, 50*	Asian-Pacific, *Singapore
Malaysia	46024	2/5/05	13	20	Malaysia
Maliha and Jade	40600	8/2/06	15	15	St. Louis Zoo
Manchu	40456	8/26/06	14	7	
Mandy	40020	7/18/02	7, 11	7, 7	
Manes	40352	10/6/05	14	7	
Manny	4081	6/8/95	3, 4	75, 50	

Manny

Maple

Marsh

Marshall

Marshmallow

Masque

Name	Style	Bday	Gen	$	Note
Maple	4600	7/1/96	4	375	Canada, "Pride" on tush tag
Maple	4600	7/1/96	4, 5	25, 25	Canada, "Maple" on tush tag
March	4390	none	10	7	potbelly
March 2003	4554	none	special	7	new face
Mardi Gras	40199	2/24/04	13	10	
Marsh	48436	5/1/07	special	8	BBOM: 5/07
Marshall	40068	2/26/04	12	150	Arlington Jr. Jockey Club
Marshall	40068	2/26/04	12	75	Arlington Park
Marshall	40068	2/26/04	12	7	
Marshmallow	40182	5/3/04	13	7	
Mary	46079	9/1/06	14	35	Verdes
Mascotte	46060	6/9/06	14	20	Europe
Masque	44044	2/8/05	13	8	Ty Store

Max

May 2003

Name	Style	Bday	Gen	$	Note
Massachusetts	40125	none	12	7	Sold only in Massachusetts
Massachusetts Mayflower	40299	none	13	10	Trade Show
Matlock	40656	6/1/07	15	7	
Mattie	4521	4/26/01	7, 10	7, 7	
Max	40606	none	15	7	Max & Ruby
May	4392	none	10	7	potbelly
May 2003	4556	none	special	7	new face
McWooly	40174	5/10/04	13	7	
Meekins	40329	5/16/05	14	7	
Mel	4162	1/14/96	4, 5	7, 7	
Melbourne	46053	none	14	20	Australia
Mellow	4344	12/7/00	7, 8	7, 7	

Mel

Mellow

Miami

Midnight

Millennium

Name	Style	Bday	Gen	$	Note
Merlion	46091	8/9/06	15	10	Asian-Pacific
Merriment	48431	12/1/06	special	8	BBOM: 12/06
Merry Kiss-mas	40276	12/30/04	13	7	
Merrybelle	40283	9/24/04	13	7	
Miami	40378	6/21/06	14	7	
Midnight	4355	12/23/00	7, 8	7, 7	
Millennium	4226	1/1/99	5	7, 7	correct/wrong spelling
Minksy	40185	6/4/04	13	7	
Minneapolis	40132	3/1/04	12	10	Trade Show
Minnesota	40119	none	12	7	Sold Only in Minnesota
Minnesota Lady's-slipper	40295	none	13	10	Trade Show
Mississippi	44079	none	13	7	$1 donated to Red Cross
Mississippi	40320	none	13	7	Ty Store: $2 donated to Red Cross
Mistletoe	4500	12/18/00	7, 9	7, 7	

Minneapolis

Mistletoe

Mom

Mom 2006

Name	Style	Bday	Gen	$	Note
Mom	40216	5/9/04	13	7	holding letters
Mom 2006	44086	5/14/06	14	7	Ty Store
Mom 2007	44103	5/13/07	15	7	Ty Store
MOM-e	4411	5/12/02	10	15	Ty Store
MOM-e 2003	4426	5/11/02	11	8	Ty Store
MOM-e 2004	4438	5/9/04	12	7	Ty Store
MOM-e 2005	44048	5/8/05	13	7	Ty Store
Monarch	47533	none	15	7	San Francisco Zoo
MONKEY	4324	none	6	7	Zodiac
Mooch	4224	8/1/98	5	7	
Moonlight	40263	5/13/05	13	7	
Moosletoe	40137	12/23/03	12	7	
Mooosly	40377	1/4/06	14	7	

MOM-e

MOM-e 2003

MONKEY

Mooch

Mooosly

Morrie

Name	Style	Bday	Gen	$	Note
Morrie	4282	2/20/00	6, 7	7, 7	
Morsel	47090	8/13/07	15	7	Walgreen's: Hersheys
Mother	4588	5/16/02	7, 11	7, 7	
Mother 2004	40059	5/11/03	12	7	
Mr.	4363	none	7, 8	7, 7	
Mr. Jeremy Fisher	46066	none	14	12	UK/Beatrix Potter
Mr. Krabs	40468	none	14	7	SpongeBob
Mr. Krabs Key-clip	47056	none	14	12	SpongeBob: Best Buy
Mr. Tod	46068	none	14	12	UK/Beatrix Potter
Mrs.	4364	none	7, 8	7, 7	
Muddy	4006	6/26/02	11	7	
Muff	40229	11/20/04	13	7	

Mother

Mr.

Mrs.

Mr. Krabs

Muddy

Mukluk

Name	Style	Bday	Gen	$	Note
Muffler	44062	12/31/05	13	7	Ty Store
Mugungwha	4617	2/12/02	10	20	Korea
Mukluk	40031	2/26/03	7, 11	8, 8	clear or blue eye/green eye
Mum	4517	5/13/01	7, 10	8, 8	UK
Mum	46028	3/6/05	13	8	Europe/Australia/ New Zealand
Muscle Man Star	40381	none	14	7	SpongeBob SquarePants
MuscleBob BuffPants	40382	none	14	7	SpongeBob SquarePants
My Dad	40612	6/17/06	15	7	
My Mom	40604	5/13/07	15	7	
My Mum	46097	3/18/07	15	10	UK/Australia

Muscle Man Star

My Mom

Mystic

My Sweet

Name	Style	Bday	Gen	$	Note
My Sweet	40723	2/14/07	15	7	
Mystery	46030	6/22/04	13	30	UK
Mystic	4007	none	1, 2, 3	2,800, 400, 200	tan horn w/fine mane
Mystic	4007	5/21/94	3, 4	150, 7	tan horn with coarse mane
Mystic	4007	5/21/94	4, 5	7, 7	iridescent horn with coarse mane
Mystic	4007	5/21/94	5	7	iridescent horn with rainbow mane
Mystique	40062	1/27/03	12	7	
N (alphabet bear)	40514	none	special	4	
Nami	44201	none	12	7	Ty Store/World Wildlife Fund
Nana	44090	9/10/06	14	7	Ty Store

Nami

Nanook

NASCAR: Casey Mears #25

NASCAR: Jeff Burton No. 31

Name	Style	Bday	Gen	$	Note
Nana (later as "Bongo")	4067	none	3	3,500	
Nana 2007	44111	9//9/07	15	7	Ty Store
Nanook	4104	11/21/96	4, 5	7, 7	
Nara	46003	1/22/04	12	15	Korea
NASCAR: Carl Edwards #99	40645	8/15/79	15	7	
NASCAR: Casey Mears #25	40562	3/12/78	15	7	
NASCAR: Clint Bowyer #07	40644	5/30/79	15	7	
NASCAR: Denny Hamlin #11	40641	11/18/80	15	7	
NASCAR: Elliott Sadler #19	40638	4/30/75	15	7	
NASCAR: Greg Biffle #16	40567	12/23/69	15	7	
NASCAR: J. J. Yeley #18	40642	10/5/76	15	7	
NASCAR: Jeff Burton No. 31	40566	6/29/67	15	7	

NASCAR: Kevin Harvick No. 29

NASCAR: Matt Kenseth #17

Name	Style	Bday	Gen	$	Note
NASCAR: Jeff Gordon #24	40635	8/4/71	15	7	
NASCAR: Jimmie Johnson #48	40636	9/17/75	15	7	(2) UK Exclusive
NASCAR: Kasey Kahne #9	40639	4/10/80	15	7	
NASCAR: Kevin Harvick No. 29	40568	12/8/75	15	7	
NASCAR: Kurt Busch #2	40564	8/4/78	15	7	
NASCAR: Kyle Busch #5	40637	5/2/85	15	7	
NASCAR: Mark Martin #01	40643	1/9/59	15	7	
NASCAR: Matt Kenseth #17	40561	3/10/72	15	7	
NASCAR: No. 3	40569	none	15	7	
NASCAR: Racer (black)	40563	7/29/07	15	7	
NASCAR: Racer (red)	40563	2/18/07	15	7	

Nascar: Racer

New Year 2008

Name	Style	Bday	Gen	$	Note
NASCAR: Racer (blue)	40563	5/27/07	15	7	
NASCAR: Ryan Newman #12	40565	12/8/77	15	7	
NASCAR: Tony Stewart #20	40640	5/20/71	15	7	UK
Nectar	4361	7/30/00	7, 8	35, 35	
Negaraku	46040	6/15/05	13	25, 50*	Asian-Pacific, *Malasia
Neon	4239	4/1/99	5	7	
Nermal	40109	none	12	8	Garfield
New Jersey	40227	12/18/1787	13	7	Sold only in New Jersey
New Year 2006	40309	12/31/05	13	7	
New Year 2007	40457	1/1/07	14	7	
New Year 2008	40718	12/31/07	15	7	
New York	40049	7/26/03	12	100	Trade Show - "I ♥ New York"
New York	40050	7/26/03	12	7	"I ♥ New York"
New York Rose	40288	none	13	10	Trade Show

Nectar

Neon

Nermal

New York

Nibbler

Name	Style	Bday	Gen	$	Note
New York State	40148	none	12	10	Sold only in New York
New Zealand	46026	1/16/05	13	20	Asian-Pacific/ New Zealand
Nibble	40494	1/6/07	15	7	
Nibbler	4216	4/6/98	5	7	frowning or smiling
Nibblies	4584	3/26/02	7, 11	7, 7	
Nibbly	4217	5/7/98	5, 5	7, 7	frowning or smiling
Nigel	46086	10/1/06	14	15	Beales
Niklas	46105	11/5/06	15	15	German
Niles	4284	2/1/00	6, 7	7, 7	
Nina	44021	10/12/04	12	7	Ty Store
Nip	4003	none	2, 3	500, 250	white face
Nip	4003	none	3	400	all gold

Nibblies

Nibbly

Niles

Nip

November

November 2002

Nutty

Oats

Name	Style	Bday	Gen	$	Note
Nip	4003	3/6/94	3, 4, 5	150, 7, 7	white paws
Nipponia	4605	9/15/00	6, 7	25, 15	Japan
Northland	46020	4/17/05	13	10	Canada
November	4386	none	10	7	potbelly
November 2002	4550	none	special	7	new face
Nuts	4114	1/21/96	4, 5	7, 7	
Nutty	4587	8/3/02	7, 11	7, 7	
O (alphabet bear)	40515	none	special	4	
Oakdale	44115	9/23/07	15	7	Ty Store
Oats	4305	7/5/00	6, 7	7, 7	
Ocker	46000	1/1/04	12	15	Asian-Pacific/Australia
October	4380	none	10	7	potbelly
October 2002	4549	none	special	7	new face
Odie	40669	none	15	7	Garfield: yellow
Odie	40112	none	12	8	Garfield: tan w/ tag

October

October 2002

Name	Style	Bday	Gen	$	Note
Odie	none	none	12	15	Garfield: mini Odie w/DVD
O'Fortune	40481	3/17/07	15	7	
Ohio	40122	none	12	7	Sold only in Ohio
Ohio Scarlet Carnation	40296	none	13	10	Trade Show
Old Timer	47002	9/26/04	12	7	Cracker Barrel
Ole'	46006	1/8/04	12	24, 125*	Europe/Spain: nobre, *nombre
O'Lucky	44101	3/17/07	15	8	Ty Store
Omnia	46113	11/3/07	none		UK Harrods, boxed
Omnia Key-clip	none	11/3/07	none	25, 40*	UK Harrods
Omnibus	46114	11/3/07	none	15	UK Harrods, boxed
Omnibus Key-clip	none	11/3/07	none	25, 40*	UK Harrods

Old Timer

O'Lucky

Opie

Ooh-La-La

Oriel

Name	Style	Bday	Gen	$	Note
Ontario White Trillium	46037	none	13	15	Trade Show
Onny	40633	9/28/07	15	20	Boblins: Canada/ Australia/N Zealand/UK
Ooh-La-La	40093	5/6/04	12	7	
Opie	40246	4/23/05	13	7	blue eyes
Opie	47007	4/23/05	13	10	Sea Center: pink eyes
Orange Ice	40678	6/23/07	15	7	Trade Show
Oriel	40249	9/28/04	13	7	
Orient	40713	7/31/07	15	7	
Orion	40019	7/21/03	7, 11	7, 7	
Osito	4244	2/5/99	5	7	USA
Outlaw	40389	1/9/06	14	7	
OX	4328	none	6	7	Zodiac

Orion

OX

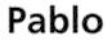

Pablo

Palace

Palms

Panama

Pappa

Pappa 2004

Name	Style	Bday	Gen	$	Note
P (alphabet bear)	40516	none	special	4	
P.F.C.	46018	9/3/04	12	15	UK: with or without box
Pablo	40412	none	13	7	*Backyardigans
Packer	46073	4/22/06	14	15	UK
Pads	46089	11/7/07	15	15	UK
Pal	44089	8/8/06	14	7	Ty Store
Palace	48435	4/1/07	special	8	BBOM: 4/07
Palms	40554	5/22/06	15	7	
Panama	4520	8/25/01	7, 10	7, 7	
Panmunjom	46094	6/24/06	15	20	Asian-Pacific: Korean map
Pansy	47041	4/21/06	15	7	Hallmark Gold Crown
Papa	44091	9/10/06	14	7	Ty Store
Papa 2007	44112	9/9/07	15	7	Ty Store
Pappa	4593	6/15/02	7, 11	7, 7	
Pappa 2004	40065	6/19/03	12	7	

Patrick Claus

Patrick Star – Best Day Ever

Name	Style	Bday	Gen	$	Note
Parka	40411	1/6/06	14	7	SpongeBob
Patrick Barnacleboy	40433	none	14	8	SpongeBob
Patrick Claus	40282	none	13	8	SpongeBob
Patrick Muscle Man Star	40381	none	14	8	SpongeBob
Patrick Star	40164	none	12	9	SpongeBob
Patrick Star - Best Day Ever	40467	none	14	8	SpongeBob
Patrick Star - Best Day Ever	47055	none	14	12	SpongeBob
Patrick Star Key-Clip	40407	none	14	6	SpongeBob: Best Buy
Patriot	4360	5/29/00	8	15	USA - flag on left foot
Patriot	4360	5/29/00	8	10	USA - flag on right foot
Patti	4025	none	1	2,800	deep fuchsia body
Patti	4025	none	1, 2	2500, 800	raspberry body
Patti	4025	none	3	500	magenta/maroon

Patriot

Patti

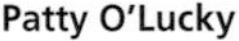

Patty O'Lucky

Peace Symbol Bear

Name	Style	Bday	Gen	$	Note
Patti	4025	1/6/93	3, 4, 5	125, 7, 7	fuchsia body
Patti	49026	1/6/93	special	50	BBOC: Original 9, set 1
Patti	49027	1/6/93	special	15	BBOC: Original 9, set 2-4
Patti	49028	1/6/93	special	10	BBOC: Original 9, set 5
Patty O'Lucky	44081	3/17/06	14	7	Ty Store
Paul	4248	2/23/1999	5	7	
Peace	4053	2/1/96	5	25 to 200	Indo
Peace	4053	2/1/96	5	7 to 150	China
Peace Symbol Bear	4599	11/17/02	11	10	UK/Singapore: hollow symbol
Peace Symbol Bear	4599	11/17/02	11	10	USA: filled-in symbol
Peanut	4062	1/25/95	3, 4, 5	200, 7, 7	light blue body
Peanut	4062	none	3	1,800	royal blue body
Pecan	4251	4/15/99	5	7	
Peekaboo	4303	4/11/00	6, 7	7, 7	

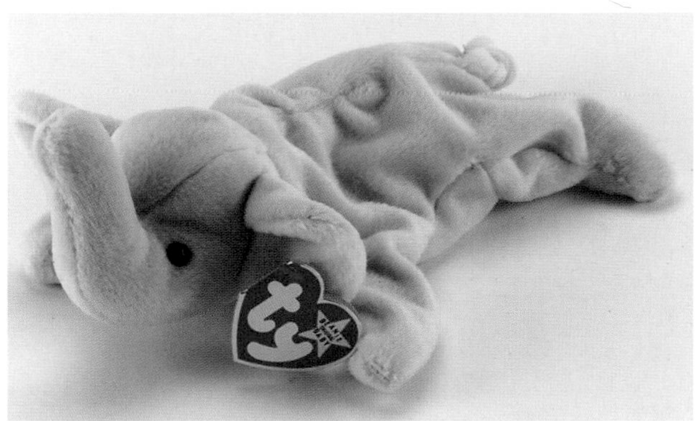

Peanut

Peekaboo

Pegasus

Peking

Pellet

Periwinkle

Petunia

Pigling Bland

Name	Style	Bday	Gen	$	Note
Peepers	4814	3/1/04	special	7	BBOM: 3/04
Peeps	40168	4/28/04	13	7	
Pegasus	4542	9/1/01	7, 10	8, 8	
Peking	4013	none	1	2,500	
Peking	4013	none	2, 3	1,000, 800	
Pellet	4313	7/29/00	6, 7	7, 7	
Pennsylvania	40084	none	12	7	Sold only in Pennsylvania
Pennsylvania Mountain Laurel	40290	none	13	10	Trade Show
Periwinkle	40345	none	14	7	Blues Clues
Periwinkle	48236	none	14	7	USPS
Periwinkle	4400	2/08/00	6	7	
Peter Rabbit	46064	none	14	12	UK/Beatrix Potter
Petunia	47041	4/21/06	15	7	Hallmark Gold Crown

Pierre

Pilgrim

Pinchers

Piñata

Pique

Name	Style	Bday	Gen	$	Note
Phantom	47070	10/28/06	15	7	Borders
Philadelphia	40126	3/11/03	12	7	Trade Show
Pi	40609	none	15	7	Boblins: Canada/ Australia/New Zealand/UK
Picnic	48439	none	special	7	BBOM: 8/07
Pierre	4607	5/4/01	9	15	Canada
PIG	4327	none	6	7	Zodiac
Pigling Bland	46067	none	14	12	UK/Beatrix Potter
Pilgrim	44120	11//22/07	15	7	Ty Store
Piñata	40051	5/5/03	12	7	black or Mexican flag nose
Pinchers	4026	6/19/93	1	2,500	
Pinchers	4026	6/19/93	3, 4, 5	350, 60, 7, 7	

Pirouette

Pluff

Name	Style	Bday	Gen	S	Note
Pinchers	49024	6/19/93	special	10	BBOC: Original 9, sets 1, 2, 3, 5
Pinkerton	40360	1/16/06	14	7	
Pinky	4072	2/13/95	3, 4, 5	50, 7, 7	
Pinny	40632	9/28/07			Boblins: Canada/ Australia/N Zealand/ UK
Pinta	44021	10/12/04	12	7	Ty Store
Pippo	46008	3/19/04	12	10	Italy/Harrods
Pique	40340	11/12/05	14	7	
Piran	46101	3/5/07	15	130	UK/Abbey Bears
Piran	46100	3/5/07	15	85	Cornish; black or flag nose
Piran	46100	3/5/07	15	25	UK/Cornish
Pirouette	40255	11/17/04	13	7	
Pittsburgh	40129	7/20/04	12	20	Trade Show
Pluff	40235	11/20/04	13	7	

Pompoms

Pooky

Name	Style	Bday	Gen	$	Note
Plymouth	40272	12/21/04	13	7	
Pocus	48417	10/1/05	special	8	BBOM: 10/05
Poet	40160	10/16/04	12	7	
Pompey	4625	8/10/02	7	25	UK Portsmouth Football Club
Pompoms	40386	2/27/06	14	7	
Ponder	40663	3/5/07	15	7	
Poochie Poo Key-clip	40671	none	15	4	
Poofie	4505	7/17/01	7, 9	8, 8	
Poofie Key-clip	40400	none	14	4	
Pooky	40155	none	12th	7	
Pooky Key-clip	40672	none	15	4	
Poolside	44110	6/21/07	15	7	Ty Store
Poopsie	4381	3/31/01	7, 9	7, 7	
Popcorn	4809	10/1/03	special	7	BBOM: 10/03

Poolside

Pops - Canadian Tie

Name	Style	Bday	Gen	$	Note
Pops	4522	6/16/01	10	8	American tie
Pops	4522	6/16/01	7	20	British tie
Pops	4522	6/16/01	10	15	Canadian tie
Poseidon	4356	9/14/00	7, 8	8, 7	
Posy	47041	4/21/06	15	7	Hallmark Gold Crown
Pouch	4161	11/6/96	4, 5	7, 7	
Pounce	4122	8/28/97	5	7	
Pounds	4530	3/30/02	7, 10	7, 7	
Prance	4123	11/20/97	5	7	
Premier	4635	8/18/02	7	25	UK Portsmouth Football Club
Pretzels	40192	10/19/04	13	9	
Prickles	4220	2/19/98	5	7	
Pride	46029	9/21/04	13	7	UK
Prima	40304	4/28/05	13	7	

Poseidon

Pouch

Pounds

Pretzels

Prance

Prickles

Prince

Propeller

Pudding

Puffer

Name	Style	Bday	Gen	$	Note
Prince	4312	7/3/00	6, 7	7, 7	
Princess	4300	none	5	7, 12*	PE pellets, PVC*
Princess	4300	none	5	45	Indo
Prinz von Gold	4613	10/3/01	7	25	Germany
Promise	47014	7/23/05	13	50	Northwestern Mutual: brown or blue
Propeller	4366	8/8/00	7, 8	7, 7	
Prunella	47016	8/1/05	13	7	Hallmark Gold Crown
Pudding	40474	11/13/06	14	7	
Puffer	4181	11/3/97	5	7	
Pugsly	4106	5/2/96	4, 5	7, 7	
Pumkin'	4205	10/31/98	5	7	
Punchers	4026	none	1st	3,000	
Punchers	49025	none	special	75	BBOC: Origninal 9, sets 4

Pugsly

Pumkin'

Pungo

PUNXSUTAWN-e Phil

Punxsutawney Phil 2004

Punxsutawney Phil 2005

Name	Style	Bday	Gen	$	Note
Punchline	44084	4/1/06	14	7	Ty Store
Pungo	44202	none	13	7	Ty Store/World Wildife Fund
PUNXSUTAWN-e PHIL	4418	2/2/02	11, 11	12, 175	Ty Store/Punx. C of C
PUNXSUTAWN-e Phil 2004	4434	2/2/04	12	7	Ty Store: light fur
PUNXSUTAWN-e Phil 2005	44039	2/2/05	13	9	Ty Store
PUNXSUTAWN-e Phil 2006	44080	2/2/06	14	7	Ty Store
PUNXSUTAWN-e Phil 2007	44099	2/2/07	15	7	Ty Store
PUNXSUTAWN-e Phil 2008	44123	2/2/08	15	7	Ty Store
Punxsutawney Phil	4418	2/2/02	11	170	Punx. C of C

Punxsutawney Phil 2008

Puppy Claus

Name	Style	Bday	Gen	$	Note
Punxsutawney Phil 2004	40034	2/2/04	12	7	dark fur
Punxsutawney Phil 2004	4705	2/2/04	12	12	Punx. C of C: light fur
Punxsutawney Phil 2005	40197	2/2/05	13	9	
Punxsutawney Phil 2005	47006	2/2/05	13	9	Punx. C. of C.
Punxsutawney Phil 2006	40326	2/2/06	14	7	
Punxsutawney Phil 2006	47022	2/2/06	14	7	Punxsutawney C of C
Punxsutawney Phil 2007	40477	2/2/07	15	7	
Punxsutawney Phil 2007	47059	2/2/07	14	12	Punxsutawney C of C
Punxsutawney Phil 2008	40722	2/2/08	15	7	
Punxsutawney Phil 2008	40722	2/2/08	15	7	Punxsutawney C of C
Pup-In-Love	40309	10/12/05	13	7	
Puppy Claus	48443	none	special	7	BBOM: 12/7, last one
Purr	4346	3/18/00	7, 8	7, 7	

Purr

Quackington

Quackers

Quivers

RABBIT

Name	Style	Bday	Gen	$	Note
Puss In Boots	47086	1/13/07	special	5	WalMart: mini in Shrek DVD
Q (alphabet bear)	40517	none	special	4	
Quacker	4024	none	2, 3	1500, 1500	no wings
Quacker	4024	none	2, 3	600, 600	w/ wings
Quackington	47084	4/8/07	15	7	Hallmark
Quackers	4024	none	1	3,000	no wings
Quackers	4024	4/19/94	3, 4, 5	75, 7, 7	w/ wings
Quebec Iris Versicolor	46036	none	13	20	Trade Show
Quiet	47064	3/2/07	15	30	Northwestern Mutual
Quivers	40018	10/22/02	7, 11	7, 7	
R (alphabet bear)	40518	none	special	4	
RABBIT	4327	none	6	7	Zodiac
Racer	40563	7/29/07	15	7	(3) red, blue, black

Rainbow

Raine

Ramble

Red

Regal

Name	Style	Bday	Gen	$	Note
Racing Gold	44119	2/17/08	15	7	Ty Store: red, gold, white, black, blue
Radar	4091	10/30/95	3, 4	80, 50	
Rainbow	4037	10/14/97	5	7	blue w/ no tongue
Rainbow	4037	10/14/97	5	7	tie-dye rainbow w/ tongue
Raine	44085	3/20/06	14	35	Ty Store
Rally Monkey	47067	6/6/00	15	50	LA Angels
Ramble	48415	8/1/05	special	7	BBOM: 8/05
RAT	4321	none	6	7	Zodiac
Ratzo	40099	4/1/04	12	7	purple
Ratzo	44059	10/31/05	13	7	Ty Store: grey
Red	40000	1/23/03	11	10	USA
Red, White & Blue	40000	7/4/02	11	10	USA
Redford	40157	8/18/04	12	7	
Reefs	40558	6/2/06	15	7	

RAT

Reefs

Rescue

Righty 2000

Name	Style	Bday	Gen	$	Note
Reese	40682	5/30/07	15	7	
Regal	4358	11/11/00	7, 8	7, 7	
Rescue	4514	none	7, 9	7, 7	flag on left or right leg
Rescue	4514	none	9	7	Ty Store - flag on right leg
Rex	4086	8/1/94	3	400	
Rhapsody	40473	8/11/06	14	7	
Ricochet	40584	5/30/07	15	7	
Riggins	48440	none	special	7	BBOM: 9/07
Righty	4086	7/4/96	4	60	USA
Righty 2000	4289	7/4/00	6	8	USA
Righty 2004	40044	6/25/03	12	7	
Ringo	4014	7/14/95	3, 4, 5	50, 7, 7	
Roam	4209	9/27/98	5	7	
Roary	4069	2/20/96	4, 5	7, 7	

Ringo

Roary

Rocket

Romance

Name	Style	Bday	Gen	$	Note
Roary	4069	none	5	1,800	given to top McDonald producers
Rocket	4202	3/12/97	5	7	
Roger	46078	8/23/06	14	35	Verdes
Romance	4398	2/2/01	7, 9	7, 7	
Romeo & Juliet	40306	2/9/05	13	10	
Ronald McDonald	47000	4/19/04	12	200	McDonald Worldwide Conventioin
Ronnie	40015	2/6/03	11	7	USA
Rooftop	40710	10/4/06	15	7	
ROOSTER	4318	none	6	6	
ROOSTER	43255	none	6	9	Zodiac
Rootbeer	40681	10/4/06	15	7	
Rose	4622	4/23/02	7	40	UK
Rover	4101	5/30/96	4, 5	7, 7	

Ronnie

ROOSTER

Rover

Roxie

Rudy

Rufus

Rumba

Rusty

Name	Style	Bday	Gen	$	Note
Rowdy	40367	6/11/05	14	7	
Roxie	4334	12/1/00	6, 7	7, 7	red or black nose
Ruby	40365	7/2/05	14	15	Red Hat Society
Ruby	40607	none	15	7	Max & Ruby; USA/Can
Ruddle	40610	none	15	7	Boblins: Can/Aust/N Zealand/UK
Rudy	40029	5/22/03	7, 11	7, 7	
Rufus	4280	2/28/00	6, 7	7, 7	
Rumba	40007	12/27/02	7, 11	7, 7	
Runner	4304	5/25/00	6	45	cobra poem
Runner	4304	5/25/00	6, 7	7, 7	ferret poem
Rusty	4563	2/18/02	7, 10	7, 7	
S (alphabet bear)	40519	none	special	4	
Saffron	40360	1/16/06	14	7	

Sakura II

Santa

Name	Style	Bday	Gen	$	Note
Sakura	4602	3/25/00	6	75	Japan
Sakura II	4619	3/3/02	10	20	Japan
Salute	40486	11/11/06	15	7	flag on chest
Salute	44104	11/11/06	15	7	Ty Store: flag on sleeve
Sam	40075	7/4/04	12	7	blue, red, or white body
Sammy	4215	6/23/98	5	7	
Sampson	4540	12/29/01	7, 10	7, 7	
San Francisco	40146	4/15/04	12	10	Trade Show
Sandals	40557	3/30/06	15	7	
Santa	4203	12/6/98	5	7	
Santa Maria	44021	10/12/04	12	7	Ty Store
Sapphire	48400	5/1/04	special	7	BBOM: 5/04
Sarge	4277	2/14/00	6, 7	7, 7	
Scaly	4263	2/9/99	5	7	
Scampy	40106	9/9/03	12	7	

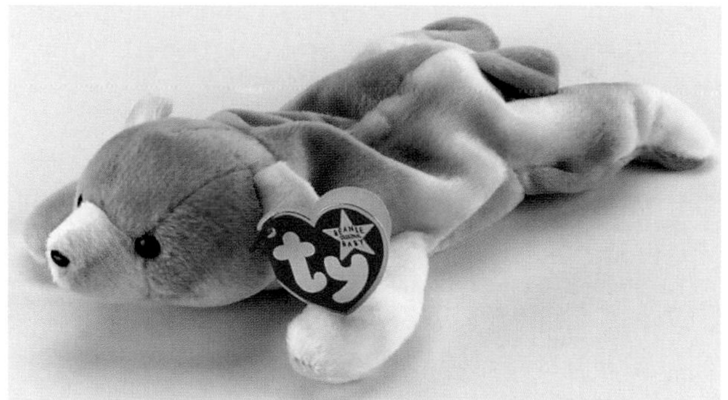

Sammy

Sampson

Sarge

Scaly

SCARED-e

Schweetheart

Scat

Schnitzel

Name	Style	Bday	Gen	$	Note
SCARED-e	4415	10/26/01	10	15	Ty Store
Scarem	40578	11/13/06	15	7	
Scares	48429	10/1/06	special	7	BBOM: 10/06
Scary	4378	10/25/00	7, 9	7, 7	
Scat	4231	5/27/98	5, 5	7, 7	frowning or smiling
Schnitzel	4578	10/15/02	7, 11	7, 7	
Scholar	40619	3/11/06	15	7	
School Rocks	40725	8/30/06	14	7	Hallmark: 3 different messages
Schweetheart	4252	1/23/99	5	7	
Scoop	4107	7/1/96	4, 5	7, 7	
Scorch	4210	7/31/98	5	7	
Scotland	4609	11/1/01	7	30	Scotland
Scotland	46013	6/22/04	12	25	UK
Scottie	4102	6/3/96	4, 5	7, 7	

Scoop

Scorch

Name	Style	Bday	Gen	$	Note
Scrappy	40102	11/11/03	12	7	gold "Ty" tush tag
Scrum	46055	11/22/03	14	15	UK
Scurry	4281	1/18/00	6, 7	7, 7	
Seadog	4566	7/22/01	7, 10	7, 7	
Seamore	4029	12/14/96	1, 2	2500, 375	
Seamore	4029	12/14/96	3, 4	80, 40	
Season's Greetings	47010	12/26/04	13	7	Hallmark
Seattle	40121	12/2/03	12	15	Trade Show
Seaweed	4080	3/19/96	3, 4, 5	50, 15, 10	
Secret	40035	1/19/03	7, 11	10, 9	

Scottie

Scurry

Seadog

Seamore

Seaweed

Secretariat 1973

Name	Style	Bday	Gen	$	Note
Secretariat 1973	40478	3/30/07	15	7	1973 Kentucky Derby Winner
Secretariat 1973	40478	3/30/07	15	15	Kentucky Derby
Senna-Kun	46046	8/31/04	13	175	Motomachi Kitamura: brown paws
Senna-Kun	46046	8/31/04	13	650	Motomachi Kitamura: pink paws
September	4372	none	10	7	potbelly
September 2002	4548	none	special	7	new face
Sequoia	4516	7/17/01	7, 10	7, 7	
Serenade	48410	4/1/05	special	7	BBOM: 4/05
Serenity	4533	2/15/02	7, 10	7, 7	
Shamrock	4338	3/17/00	7, 8	7, 7	
ShaqBear	40372	3/6/06	14	7	
Shasta	40070	5/23/03	12	7	
Sheba	46119	11/3/07	15	25	Harrods UK

September

September 2002

Sequoia

Serenity

Shamrock

Sheets

Sherbert

Sherwood

Name	Style	Bday	Gen	$	Note
Sheets	4260	10/31/99	5	7	
Sheldon J. Plankton	40664	8/31/07	15	7	
Sherbet	4560	11/26/01	7, 10	7, 7	light pink, green or yellow body
Sherbet	40004	8/2/02	7, 11	7, 7	light blue or lilac body
Sherbet	40004	8/2/02	7, 11	7, 10	hot pink body
Sherwood	40023	9/8/02	7, 11	7, 7	
Shiloh	44208	none	14	20	Ty Store: World Wildlife Fund
Shivers	40115	10/30/03	12	7	
Shocks	40600	5/24/06	15	7	
Shooting Star (gray)	46048	11/5/05	13	65, 95*	Harrods UK, boxed*
Shooting Star (white)	46047	11/5/05	13	45, 65*	Harrods UK, boxed*

Siam

Silver

Shudders

Side-Kick

Name	Style	Bday	Gen	$	Note
Shortstop	40252	4/3/05	13	7	
Shudders	40418	9/20/05	14	7	
Siam	4369	10/19/00	7, 9	7, 7	
Siberia	40622	1/31/07	15	7	
Side-Kick	4532	1/30/02	7, 10	7, 7	
Siesta	4439	7/31/03	12	8	Ty Store
Silent Night Star	40691	none	15	7	Sponge Bob SquarePants
Silver	4242	2/11/99	5	7	
Silver	46001	2/7/04	12	15	Asian-Pacific/New Zealand
Singabear	4630	8/9/02	11	15	Singapore
Singapore	46023	2/9/05	13	15	Asian-Pacific/ Singapore

Sizzle

Skis

Name	Style	Bday	Gen	$	Note
Sis	44017	8/5/03	12	7	Ty Store
Sizzle	4399	8/25/01	7, 9	7, 7	
Skips	44083	4/16/06	14	10	Ty Store
Skis	40438	2/13/06	14	7	
Slamdunk	40414	12/30/05	14	7	
Slapshot	40618	10/27/06	15	7	
Slayer	4307	9/26/00	6, 7	7, 7	
Sledge	4538	4/26/02	7, 10	7, 7	
Sleighbelle	40144	6/5/04	12	7	green or white
Sleighride	40708	11/11/06	15	7	
Slick	40072	8/11/03	12	7	
Slippery	4222	1/17/98	5	7	
Slither	4031	none	1, 2, 3	2500, 1000, 800	

Slayer

Sledge

Slippery

Smart

Sly

Smarter

Smartest

Name	Style	Bday	Gen	$	Note
Slowpoke	4261	5/20/99	5	7	
Slush Key-clip	40677	none	15	4	
Sly	4115	9/12/96	4	50	brown belly
Sly	4115	9/12/96	4, 5	8, 7	white belly
Smart	4353	6/7/00	7, 8	7, 7	
Smarter	4526	6/12/01	7, 10	7, 7	
Smartest	4591	6/9/02	7, 11	7, 7	
Smarty	40232	4/13/04	13	7	
Smarty	44050	4/29/05	13	7	Ty Store
Smarty Jones	40698	2/28/01	15	7	2004 Kentucky Derby Winner
Smash	40270	8/29/05	13	10	U.S. Open: gold logo
Smash	47011	8/29/05	13	225	U.S. Open: silver logo

Smitten

Smooch

Name	Style	Bday	Gen	$	Note
Smitten	4577	2/16/02	7, 11	7, 7	black or pink nose
Smooch	4335	2/14/00	7, 8	10, 10	
SMOOCH-e	4435	2/14/04	12	10	Ty Store
Smoochy	4039	10/1/97	5	7	thread or felt mouth
Smudges	40225	8/4/04	13	7	
Snacks	40583	8/26/07	15	7	
SNAKE	4325	none	6	7	Zodiac
Sneakers	40461	10/26/06	14	7	
Sneaks	40712	6/26/07	15	7	
Sneaky	4278	2/22/00	6, 7	7, 7	
Sniffer	4299	5/6/00	6, 7	7, 7	
Snip	4120	10/22/96	4, 5	7, 7	
Snips	49008	1/31/04	12	12, 25*	BBOC: with box*
Snocap	4573	11/8/01	7, 10	8, 8	

Smoochy

SNAKE

Sneaky

Sniffer

Snort

Snips

Snocap

Name	Style	Bday	Gen	$	Note
Snocap	4573	11/8/01	7, 10	75, 75	Brookfield Zoo
Snookums	40261	10/13/04	13	7	
Snoops	40244	10/20/04	13	7	
Snoopy	47068	6/1/07	15	10	Knott's Berry Farm
Snoopy	47078	6/1/07	15	10	Camp Snoopy
Snort	4002	5/15/95	4, 5	7, 7	
Snowball	4201	12/22/96	4	7	
Snowbelles	47028	12/1/06	14	12	Hallmark: white or red
Snowdrift	40026	12/29/02	7, 11	7, 7	
Snowdrop	44095	12/22/06	14	7	Ty Store
Snowgirl	4333	11/30/00	6, 7	7, 7	
Snuggins	48433	2/1/07	special	7	BBOM: 2/07
Soar	4410	7/4/01	10	8	Ty Store
Soar Key-clip	40369	none	14	4	

Snowdrift

Snuggins

Sonnet

Sparkles

Sparky

Speckles

Name	Style	Bday	Gen	$	Note
SoftBank HAWKS	46098	1/28/05	15	2,800	Club HAWKS
Sonnet	40036	2/19/03	7, 11	7, 7	
South Carolina	40301	none	13	7	Sold only in South Carolina
Soybean	40615	1/3/07	15	7	
Spangle	4245	6/14/99	5	7	blue, pink, or white face
Spangle Key-clip	40370	none	14	4	
Sparklers	44107	7/4/07	15	7	Ty Store
Sparkles	4800	1/1/03	10	7	BBOM: 1/03
Sparks	4633	11/5/02	7	15	UK
Sparky	4100	2/27/96	4	40, 55*	*w/ Dotty tush tag
Speckles	4402	2/17/00	6	7	Ty Store
Speedster	40183	11/16/04	13	12	
Speedy	4030	8/14/94	1	2,500	

Speedy

Spike

Spikey

Splotches

SpongeBob FrankenStein

Name	Style	Bday	Gen	$	Note
Speedy	4030	8/14/94	2, 3, 4	300, 75, 7	
Spells	44094	10/31/06	14	7	Ty Store
Spike	4060	8/13/96	4, 5	7, 7	
Spikey	40716	9/5/07	15	7	
Spinner	4036	10/28/96	5	60	Creepy on tush tag
Spinner	4036	10/28/96	4,5	7, 7	Spinner on tush tag
Splash	4022	7/8/93	1, 2	1400, 250	
Splash	4022	7/8/93	3, 4	80, 40	
Splash	49020	7/8/93	special	10	BBOC: Original 9, sets 1-5
Splotches	40715	3/9/07	15	7	
SpongeBob - Best Day Ever	40466	none	14	8	
SpongeBob - Best Day Ever	47054	none	14	12	Best Buy

SpongeBob JollyElf

SpongeBob PumpkinMask

Name	Style	Bday	Gen	$	Note
SpongeBob BuffPants	40382	none	14	8	Ty Store
SpongeBob FrankenStein	40257	none	13	9	
SpongeBob JingleBells	40690	none	15	7	SpongeBob SquarePants
SpongeBob JollyElf	40281	none	13	8	
SpongeBob SquarePants Key-clip	40406	none	14	4	Ty Store
SpongeBob Mermaidman	40432	none	14	8	Ty Store
SpongeBob PinkPants	40416	none	14	8, 12*	Ty Store, UK, *Canada
SpongeBob PumpkinMask	40258	none	13	9	
SpongeBob QB	40462	none	14	8	Ty Store
SpongeBob SleighRide	40280	none	13	8	
SpongeBob SquarePants	40163	none	12	8	
SpongeBob - Stuck on You	40623	none	15	8	Ty Store
SpongeBob ThumbsUp	40217	none	13	8	Ty Store
SpongeBob TuxedoPants	40218	none	13	8	Ty Store

SpongeBob QB

SpongeBob TuxedoPants

Sport

Spring

Name	Style	Bday	Gen	$	Note
Spook	4090	none	3	450	
Spooky	4090	10/31/95	3, 4	80, 10	
Sport	4590	9/2/02	7, 11	7, 7	
Spot	4000	none	1, 2	2800, 1500	no spot
Spot	4000	1/3/93	2, 3, 4	900, 75, 7	with spot
Spot (no spot)	49023	none	special	100	BBOC: Orig 9, set 1
Spot (with spot)	49022	1/3/93	special	10	BBOC: Orig 9, sets 1, 3, 4, 5
Spotter	40354	12/7/05	14	7	
Spring	4513	3/7/01	7, 10	7, 7	
Springfield	40053	6/18/03	12	7	
Springston	40601	3/19/06	15	7	
Springy	4272	2/29/00	6, 7	7, 7	

Spot

Spunky

Star

Stargazer

Name	Style	Bday	Gen	$	Note
Spuds	40191	7/6/04	13	8	
Spunky	4184	1/14/97	5	7	
Squealer	4005	4/23/93	1, 2	2500, 350	
Squealer	4005	4/23/93	3, 4, 5	50, 7, 7	
Squealer	49017	4/23/93	special	10	BBOC: Orig 9, sets 1-5
Squidward Tentacles	40165	none	12	9	
Squirmy	4302	4/13/00	6, 7	7, 7	
Star	4703	11/19/03	11	12	Ideation: blue star
Star	40030	11/19/03	7, 11	8, 8	gold star
Star	40030	11/19/03	11	50	Bon Ton/Elder-Beerman (gold star)
Starboard	40396	6/13/06	14	7	
Stargazer	40459	10/8/06	14	7	

Stinger

Stinky

Name	Style	Bday	Gen	$	Note
Starlett	4382	1/9/01	7, 9	7, 7	
Starlight	46010	11/6/03	12	25, 60*	Harrods UK: black, boxed*
Starlight	46011	11/6/03	12	120, 200	Harrods UK: white, boxed*
Starry	46042	1/20/05	13	50	Australia: flag nose
Starry	46042	1/20/05	13	10	Asian-Pacific: black nose
Steg	4087	11/1/94	3	450	
Stilts	4221	6/16/98	5	7	
Sting	4077	8/27/95	3, 4	75, 50	
Stinger	4193	9/29/97	5	7	
Stinky	4017	2/13/95	3, 4, 5	50, 8, 7	
Stirring	40707	12/12/06	15	7	

Street Sense

Stripey

Name	Style	Bday	Gen	$	Note
Stockings	40140	11/26/03	12	7	
Stony	44204	none	13	10	Ty Store/World Wildlife Fund
Street Sense	40697	2/23/04	15	7	2007 Kentucky Derby Winner
Stretch	4182	9/21/97	5	7	
Stripers	40353	11/5/05	14	7	
Stripes	4065	none	3	175	orange stripes
Stripes	4065	none	3	400	orange stripes w/ fuzzy belly
Stripes	4065	6/11/95	4, 5	10, 7	tan stripes
Stripey	40256	1/8/05	13	7	
Stripey Key-clip	40675	none	15	4	
Strut	4171	3/8/96	4, 5	7, 7	
Stubby	40180	1/20/04	13	7	
Stuffed	48430	11/1/06	special	9	BBOM: 11/06
Stuffings	48418	11/1/05	special	8	BBOM: 11/05
Sugar-Pie	40159	6/25/04	12	7	extra colors?

Stubby

Stuffings

Summertime Fun

Sunnie

Sunny

Sunray

Name	Style	Bday	Gen	$	Note
Sugarpup	40485	9/21/06	15	7	
Summerfest	47069	6/28/07	15	7	Milwaukee
Summertime Fun	40426	none	14	10	Chicago Show: pink
Summertime Fun	40427	none	14	10	Atlanta Show: green
Summertime Fun	40428	none	14	10	Dallas Show: orange
Summertime Fun	40429	none	14	10	Toronto Show: purple
Summertime Fun	40430	none	14	10	Los Angeles Show: yellow
Summertime Fun	40431	none	14	10	New York Show: blue
Summit	40688	7/27/07	15	7	
Sunbonnet	40324	4/24/06	14	7	
Sunburst	40553	6/4/06	15	7	
Sundar	44203	none	12	12	Ty Store/World Wildlife Fund

Sweeper

Sweetiepaws

Name	Style	Bday	Gen	$	Note
Sungoliath	46070	8/29/03	14	40	Suntory Sungoliath
Sunnie	40555	4/4/06	15	7	aqua or purple
Sunny	4401	2/13/00	6	7	
Sunray	4598	8/5/02	7, 11	7, 7	
Sunrise	40551	8/29/06	15	7	
Sunrise Key-clip	40560	none	15	4	
Sunset	40556	7/18/06	15	7	
Superstition	40419	10/13/06	14	7	
Surfin'	48437	6/1/07	special	7	BBOM: 6/07
Swampy	4273	1/24/00	6, 7	7, 7	
Sweeper	40254	10/23/04	13	7	
Sweetiekins	47019	10/14/05	14	7	Hallmark
Sweetiepaws	44093	10/21/06	14	7	Ty Store

Swirly

Swoop

Tabs

Tasha

Tasty

Name	Style	Bday	Gen	$	Note
Sweetling	44114	10/20/07	15	7	Ty Store
Swinger	40098	10/22/03	12	7	
Swinger Key-clip	40676	none	15	4	
Swiper	40728	15		7	Dora the Explorer
Swirly	4249	3/10/99	5	7	
Swoop	4268	2/24/00	6, 7	7, 7	
T (alphabet bear)	40520	none	special	4	
Tabasco	4002	5/15/95	3, 4	80, 50	
Tabbles	40605	7/5/06	15	7	
Tabs	4571	9/17/01	7, 10	7, 7	
Tanahairku	46092	10/31/06	15	20	Asian-Pacific
Tangles	4901	1/29/03	7, 11	7, 7	
Tank	4031	2/22/95	4	200	9 plates with no shell
Tank	4031	2/22/95	3, 4	175, 150	7 plates with no shell
Tank	4031	2/22/95	4	15	9 plates with shell
Tasha	40405	none	14	7	*Backyardigans
Tasty	40275	9/6/05	13	7	

Teddy (magenta with new face)

TED-e

Name	Style	Bday	Gen	$	Note
Teddy	4347	1/20/02	7, 10	39,670	100th Year Anniversary
Teddy	4050	11/28/95	2, 3, 4	800, 150, 40	brown with new face
Teddy	4050	none	1, 2	1500, 1100	brown with old face
Teddy	4052	none	2, 3	850, 825	cranberry with new face
Teddy	4052	none	1, 2	1500, 1100	cranberry with old face
Teddy	4057	none	2, 3	850, 825	jade with new face
Teddy	4057	none	1, 2	1500, 1100	jade with old face
Teddy	4056	none	2, 3	925, 900	magenta with new face
Teddy	4056	none	1, 2	1500, 1100	magenta with old face
Teddy	4051	none	2, 3	850, 825	teal with new face
Teddy	4051	none	1, 2	1500, 1100	teal with old face
Teddy	4055	none	2, 3	925, 900	violet with new face
Teddy	4055	none	1, 2	1500, 1100	violet with old face
TED-e	4414	8/19/02	10	7	Ty Store
Teegra	40659	12/27/06	15	7	

Teegra

Thanks a Bunch

The Beginning

The End

TIGER

Ticklish

Name	Style	Bday	Gen	$	Note
Tender	40167	2/10/04	13	7	
Tennessee	40226	6/1/1796	13	7	Sold only in Tennessee
Texas	40082	12/29/03	12	7	Trade Show
Texas Bluebonnet	40289	none	13	7	Trade Show
Thanks a Bunch	40531	none	14	7	
Thank You Bear	4330	none	6, 7	100, 100	Retailer
Thank You Bear	40040	none	7, 8	35, 35	Retailer
Thank You Bear	4815	4/1/04	special	7	BBOM: 4/04
Thankful	44098	11/23/06	14	7	
The Beginning	4267	6/1/02	6	7	
The End	4265	none	5	7	
Thistle	4623	11/30/01	7	35	UK
Thomas	40239	4/13/1743	13	7	
Thunderbolt	40408	2/16/06	14	7	

Tidings

Timbers

Name	Style	Bday	Gen	$	Note
Thunderbolt Key-clip	40673	none	15	4	
Tibby	40253	12/14/04	13	7	
Ticklish	40497	12/16/06	15	7	
Tidings	4431	12/22/02	11	12	Ty Store
TIGER	4320	none	6	7	Zodiac
Tiggs	40658	5/26/07	15	7	
Tiki	40631	4/17/07	15	7	
Timbers	46103	7/1/06	15	7	Canada
Tinsel	4811	12/1/03	special	8	BBOM: 12/03
Tiny	4234	9/8/98	5	7	
Tiny Tim	44028	12/25/04	12	7	Ty Store
Tipsy	40067	1/7/04	12	7	
Tiptoe	4241	1/8/99	5	7	
Titan	40251	8/17/05	13, 13	7, 25*	*Knott's Berry Farm

Tiptoe

Toast

Name	Style	Bday	Gen	$	Note
To Brighten Your Day	40533	none	14	7	
Toast	1984	2/16/03	11	7	Trade Show
Toboggan	40032	12/31/02	7, 11	7, 7	
Tom Kitten	46065	none	14	12	UK/Beatrix Potter
TOM-e	4430	11/27/03	11	7	Ty Store
Tommy	40024	11/21/02	7, 11	7, 7	
Tooter	4559	4/17/02	7, 10	7, 7	
Toothy	4523	7/10/01	7, 10	8, 8	
Tootoot	40441	3/10/06	14	7	
Topspin	47077	8/27/07	15	7	
Toronto	46016	5/25/04	12	15	Canada
Tortuga	48426	7/1/06	special	8	BBOM: 7/06
TOUR Teddy	40437	2/1/06	14	7	North America PGA
Tracker	4198	6/5/97	5	7	
Tracks	4507	10/5/01	7,10	7, 7	

Tom Kitten

Toothy

Tracks

Tradee

Tricks

Tricky

Name	Style	Bday	Gen	$	Note
Tradee	4403	6/29/00	9	7	Ty Store: "check it out" poem
Tradee 2000	4403	6/29/00	6	300	Ty Store: "buy and sell" poem
Trap	4042	none	1	2,500	
Trap	4042	none	2, 3	1000, 850	
Treehouse	40711	7/12/07	15	7	
Tremble	44116	10/31/07	15	7	Ty Store
Trick R. Treat	40420	10/31/06	14	7	
Tricks	4311	5/14/00	6, 7	7, 7	
Tricky	40017	11/15/02	7, 11	7, 7	
Trident	48413	6/1/05	special	7	BBOM: 6/05
True	4636	7/1/03	11	15	Canada
True Key-clip	46074	none	14	6	Canada
Truly	40162	11/3/04	12	7	

True

Tumba

TURK-e

Twitterbug

Tyranno

Name	Style	Bday	Gen	$	Note
Trumpet	4276	2/11/00	6, 7	7, 7	
Tubbo	4597	1/16/03	7, 11	7, 7	
Tuck	4076	9/18/95	4	75	Tusk on tush tag
Tuffy	4108	10/12/96	4, 5	7, 7	
Tumba	40649	4/8/07	15	7	Canada
Tundra	40355	9/4/05	14	7	
Tunnels	40233	7/28/05	13	7	
TURK-e	4416	11/23/01	10	10	Ty Store
Tusk	4076	9/18/95	3, 4	75, 40	
Tux	40214	12/5/04	13	7	
Twigs	4068	5/19/95	3, 4, 5	60, 7, 7	
Twilight	40105	8/3/04	12	7	
Twirls	40169	1/5/04	13	7	
Twitch	40108	8/2/03	12	30	
Twitch Key-clip	40674	none	15	4	

Uncle Sam

Valentina

Name	Style	Bday	Gen	$	Note
Twitterbug	4580	9/24/02	7, 11	7, 7	
Ty 2K	4262	1/1/00	5	7	
Tyranno	40717	5/22/07	15	7	
Tyrone	40313	none	13	7	Backyardigans
U (alphabet bear)	40521	none	special	4	
U.S.A.	4287	7/4/00	6	7	USA
Uncle Sam	40621	7/4/07	15	7	blue, red, or white nose
Union	40081	8/1/03	12	7	black or flag nose
Union	40081	8/1/03	12	25	Knott's Berry Farm
Uniqua	40311	none	13	7	Backyardigans
Unity	4606	9/28/00	7, 8	15, 15	Europe
U.S.A.	4287	7/4/00	6	7	USA
U.S.A Key-clip	40371	none	6	4	
V (alphabet bear)	40522	none	special	4	

Valentino

Veggies

Name	Style	Bday	Gen	$	Note
Valentina	4233	2/14/98	5	7	
Valentine	40038	2/14/03	7, 11	7, 7	
Valentino	4058	2/14/94	2	3,500	
Valentino	4058	2/14/94	3, 4, 5	150, 7, 7	
Valor	4433	9/11/03	11	7	Ty Store
Vanda	4614	2/18/02	10	15	Singapore
Vegas	40063	12/10/03	12	7	
Veggies	40322	3/20/06	14	7	
Velvet	4064	12/16/95	3, 4	60, 10	
Victory	44020	7/9/04	12	7	Ty Store
Villager	46032	7/1/05	13	7	
Villager Key-clip	46076	none	14	4	
Violetta	40360	1/16/06	14	7	
Virunga	4805	6/1/03	special	7	BBOM: 6/03

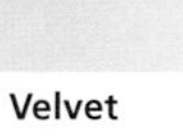

Velvet

Victory

Virunga

Waddle

We Do

Weaver

Webley

Weenie

Whiskers

Name	Style	Bday	Gen	$	Note
W (alphabet bear)	40523	none	special	4	
Waddle	4075	12/19/95	3, 4, 5	60, 7, 7	
Wailea	40379	6/21/06	14	7	
Wales	4610	9/23/01	7	20	Wales
Wales	46012	10/27/03	12	30	UK
Wallace	4264	1/25/99	5	7	
Washington	40133	none	12	7	Sold only in Washington
Washington D.C	40078	12/1/03	12	7	Trade Show
Washington Rhododendron	40297	none	13	10	Trade Show
Wattlie	4616	1/26/02	10	20	Australia
Waves	4084	12/8/96	4, 5	7, 7	
Waves	4084	12/8/96	4, 5	10, 10	Echo tush tag
We Do	40219	none	13	7	

Willoughby

Wisconsin

Name	Style	Bday	Gen	$	Note
Weaver	40250	12/13/04	13	7	
Weaver	40250	12/13/04	13	25	Knott's Berry Farm
Weaver	40250	12/13/04	13	50	Brookfield Zoo
Web	4041	none	1	2,800	
Web	4041	none	2, 3	1000, 800	
Webley	40484	8/27/06	15	7	
Weenie	4013	7/20/95	3, 4, 5	60, 8, 7	
Whiffles	40679	9/29/06	15	7	
Whiskers	4317	8/6/00	6, 7	7, 7	
Whisper	4194	4/5/97	5	7	
White	4423	4/13/03	11	7	Ty Store
Whittle	40096	11/19/03	12	7	
Wiggly	4275	1/25/00	6, 7	7, 7	

Wisest

X Alphabet Bear

Name	Style	Bday	Gen	$	Note
Wilbur	40449	none	14	7	Charlotte's Web
Wilbur	47061	none	15	7	Charlotte's Web: Walmart w/ DVD
William	4632	4/23/1564	7	25	UK: closed book
William	4632	4/23/1564	7	25	German: open book
William	46081	9/1/06	14	30	Hamley's
Willoughby	40188	7/25/04	13	7	
Winksy	40195	6/4/04	13	7	
Winstar	46071	10/8/98	14	30	Japan
Wirabear	4631	8/31/02	11	20	Malaysia
Wisconsin	40287	none	13	7	Sold only in Wisconsin
Wise	4187	5/31/97	5	7	
Wiser	4238	6/4/99	5	7	
Wisest	4286	6/6/02	6, 7	7, 7	

Yam Yam

You're Special

Name	Style	Bday	Gen	$	Note
Wish	4594	12/5/02	7, 11	7, 7	
Witchy	40577	11/10/06	15	7	
Wonton	40657	3/21/07	15	7	
Woody	4539	1/28/02	7, 10	7, 7	
Woolins	44047	3/17/05	13	7	Ty Store
Wrinkles	4103	5/1/96	4, 5	7, 7	
X (alphabet bear)	40524	none	special	4	
Y (alphabet bear)	40525	none	special	4	
Y Ddraig Goch	46031	4/24/04	13	25	UK
Y Ddraig Goch Key-clip	46104	none	15	6	UK
Yam Yam	40611	none	14	7	Boblins: Can/Aust/N Zealand/UK
Yapper	40103	3/14/04	12	7	
Yikes	47026	10/31/06	14	7	Hallmark
Yokohama	46052	none	14	7	Japan

Zoom

Zoomer

Name	Style	Bday	Gen	$	Note
You Did It	40535	none	14	7	
You're a Sweetie	40536	none	14	7	
You're Special	44055	11/2/04	13	7	Ty Store
Yours Truly	4701	12/28/02	11	7	Hallmark
Yummy	40275	9/6/05	13	7	
Z (alphabet bear)	40526	none	special	4	
Zero	4207	1/2/98	5	7	
Zeus	4589	10/23/02	7, 11	7, 7	
Ziggy	4063	12/24/95	4, 5	7, 7	
Ziggy	4063	12/24/95	3, 4	60, 7	thin stripes
Zip	4004	none	3	400	all black with pink ears
Zip	4004	none	2, 3	575, 250	white face
Zip	4004	3/28/94	3, 4, 5	150, 9, 8	white paws
Zoom	4545	9/19/01	7, 10	7, 7	
Zoomer	48421	2/1/06	special	8	BBOM: 2/06

Top Row: Quackly, Luckier, Purry, Eggs, Pico

Bottom Row: Baabet, Woolsy

Ty Beanie Babies 2.0

The 2008 generation of Beanie Babies have added new excitement to the Ty Beanie Baby line. The hang tags sport a large holographic Ty on the front and have a secret code that allows the buyer to access special activities on the designated Web site, where the Beanies take on an animated life full of adventures. Each Beanie has a blue button on its tush with a lightning bolt and "ty.com" on it. It also has an extra

Tush Button

Extra Hang Tag

blue hang tag that says "Play online!"

Duchess

Fluffball

Name	Style	Bday	Gen	$	Note
Baabet	42007	4/17/07	16	8	1st set
Duchess	42004	4/2/07	16	7	1st set
Eggs 2008	42008	3/23/08	16	7	1st set
Fluffball	42002	5/31/07	16	7	1st set
Hopsy	42010	4/3/07	16	7	1st set
Jumps	42003	7/5/07	16	7	Ty Store
Love to Mom	42014	2/29/08	16, 16	7, 10	US/UK
Luckier	42011	3/17/07	16	7	1st set
Motherly	47096	5/11/08	16	7	Hallmark
Pico	42005	6/17/07	16	7	1st set
Purry	42001	8/17/07	16	7	1st set
Quackly	42009	3/19/07	16	7	1st set
Rascal	42006	3/23/07	16	7	1st set
Shearsly	42007	5/7/07	16	8	1st set
Woolsy	42007	3/31/07	16	8	1st set

Hopsy

Jumps

Rascal

Shearsly

Ty Beanie Boppers

Top Row: Dazzlin' Destiny, Loveable Lulu, Pretty Patti, Jazzy Jessie
Bottom Row: Rugged Rusty, Bubbly Betty, Holiday Heidi

Ty introduced the first six Beanie Boppers in 2001. These figures are modeled after children and incorporate various personalities. They have interests in sports, music, and their families. Most of them are dressed in hip fashions, and some are dressed in sports team uniforms. Boppers had their own profiles listed on the Ty Web site, revealing information such as their hometowns, pets, favorite school subjects, and other personal interests. All Beanie Boppers have 1st Generation hang tags.

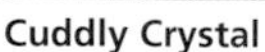

Cuddly Crystal

Dazzlin' Destiny

Name	Style	Intro	Gen	$	Note
Adorable Annie	221	2/28/02	1	9	
Boppin' Bobbi	239	7/31/03	1	8	
Bronx Bomber	100	8/5/01	1	60	New York Yankees
Bubbly Betty	207	10/1/01	1	8	
Christmas Carol	232	9/30/02	1	8, 7	green, white pompom
Cool Cassidy	215	12/27/01	1	7	
Cubbie Kerry	106	6/1/02	1	60	Chicago Cubs
Cuddly Crystal	109	9/24/01	1	10	BBOC
Cute Candy	222	4/30/02	1	9	
Dainty Darla	236	12/27/02	1	8	
Darling Debbie	219	2/28/02	1	8	

Festive Frannie

Glitzy Gabby

Name	Style	Intro	Gen	$	Note
Dazzlin' Destiny	206	9/3/01	1	9	
Elegant Ellie	238	7/31/03	1	10	
Fastball Freddie	107	9/7/02	1	60	New York Yankees
Festive Frannie	240	9/30/03	1	8	
Flirty Francie	211	12/27/01	1	9	
Footie	102	8/15/01	1	15	UK
Fun Phoebe	235	12/27/02	1	8	
Giggly Gracie	220	2/28/02	1	9	
Glitzy Gabby	218	12/27/01	1	9	
Happy Hanna	227	6/28/02	1	9	
Hat Trick Hunter	104	11/1/01	1, 1	12, 12	Canada: 10 jersey, 99 jersey

Huggable Holly

Jolly Janie

Name	Style	Intro	Gen	$	Note
Heavenly Heather	238	9/30/03	1	10	
Holiday Heidi	212	10/1/01	1	12	
Home Run Harry	108	8/10/02	1	60	Houston Astros
Huggable Holly	203	7/3/01	1	9	
Ivy Leaguer	101	9/30/01	1	60	Chicago Cubs
Jammin' Jenna	224	4/30/02	1	9	
Jazzy Jessie	209	10/1/01	1	8	
Jolly Janie	210	10/1/01	1	12	
Kooky Kandy	202	7/3/01	1	7	
Loveable Lulu	204	7/3/01	1	7	
Lovely Lily	223	4/30/02	1	8	
Lucky Lucy	229	8/29/02	1	8	

Merry Margaret

Pretty Patti

Name	Style	Intro	Gen	$	Note
Merry Margaret	231	9/30/02	1	8	
Naughty Natalie	233	9/30/02	1	8	
Paisley Payton	241	7/31/03	1	11	
Pajama Pam	234	12/27/02	1	8	
Paula Plappertasche	103	1/15/02	1	20	Germany
Precious Pammy	228	8/29/02	1	10	
Precious Penny	226	6/28/02	1	9	
Pretty Patti	205	7/3/01	1	8	
Pretty Penelope	213	12/27/01	1	8	
Punky Penny	237	7/31/03	1	8	
Rah-Rah Rachel	245	12/30/03	1	10	

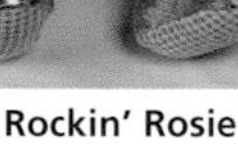

Rockin' Rosie

Sassy Star

Name	Style	Intro	Gen	$	Note
Rockin' Rosie	200	7/3/01	1	7	
Rugged Rusty	214	12/27/01	1	10	
Sassy Sidney	247	12/30/03	1	10	
Sassy Star	201	7/3/01	1	10	
Silly Sara	225	6/28/02	1	10	
Snazzy Sabrina	216	12/27/01	1	10	
Spunky Sammie	217	12/27/01	1	8	
Star-Spangled Suzy	242	7/31/03	1	8	USA
Striker	105	5/2/02	1	25, 20	UK: gold, white boots
Sweet Sally	208	10/1/01	1	8	
Totally Trish	246	12/30/03	1	8	

Ty Beanie Buddies

Top Row: Billionaire, Ariel, Osito, Hippie
Bottom Row: Siam, Cheeks, Frolic

Beanie Buddies entered the market in 1998 as larger versions of Beanie Babies. They were also softer and have more vibrant colors, sporting Ty's specially developed and patented fabric called Tylon. Several of them have been produced in large, extra-large, and jumbo sizes, challenging collectors to collect the entire "family." The Beanie Buddy series remains one of Ty's most popular.

2006 Holiday Teddy

Admiral

Name	Style	Intro	Gen	$	Note
#1 Bear	9474	12/27/02	4	11	
1997 Holiday Teddy	9426	10/1/01	4	11	
1997 Holiday Teddy	9053	10/1/01	4	11	large
1997 Holiday Teddy	9054	10/1/01	4	11	extra large
1998 Holiday Teddy	9467	9/30/02	4	11	
1999 Holiday Teddy	9468	9/30/02	4	11	
2000 Signature Bear	9348	1/4/00	4	11	
2001 Holiday Teddy	9427	10/1/01	4	11	
2002 Holiday Teddy	9701	9/30/03	4	11	
2003 Holiday Teddy	90013	9/30/04	4	11	
2005 Holiday Teddy	90040	9/30/05	4	11	
2006 Holiday Teddy	90061	9/29/06	4	11	

Name	Style	Intro	Gen	$	Note
2006 Year of the Dog	96222	11/30/05	4	11	Asian-Pacific
Aberdeen	90084	6/29/07	4	11	
Addison	9454	5/31/02	4	11	
Admiral	90053	6/30/06	4	11	
Admiral	90096	9/28/07	4	25	large
Ai	9616	11/10/03	4	20	Asian-Pacific
Almond	9425	7/31/01	4	11	
Always	90043	11/30/05	4	11	
Amber	9341	8/31/99	3	11	
America	9469	8/29/02	4	11	blue body
America	9469	8/29/02	4	11	red w/blue right ear
America	9469	8/29/02	4	11	red w/reversed ears
America	9469	8/29/02	4	11	white w/reversed ears
America	9469	8/29/02	4	11	white w/right blue ear
Ariel	9409	4/1/01	4	11	
Aussiebear	9618	11/10/03	4	20	Asian-Pacific
Avalon	90032	6/30/05	4	11	
Baby Boy	9479	12/27/02	4	11	
Baby Girl	9480	12/27/02	4	11	
Baldy	9408	4/1/01	4	11	
Bananas	9402	1/1/01	4	11	
BAT-e	90009	8/30/04	4	11	
Batty	9379	6/24/00	4, 4	120, 11	black, brown body
B.B. Bear	9398	1/1/01	4	11	
Beak	9301	9/30/98	1, 2	11, 11	
Beani	9471	10/30/02	4	11	
Benjamin	90051	4/28/06	4	11	
Billionaire	9470	9/30/02	4	12	
Blessed	90002	4/29/04	4	11	
Bloom	9719	2/26/04	4	11	
Blue	90001	4/29/04	4	11	
Blue	90056	8/31/06	4	11	Blue's Clues/TY Store

B.B. Bear

Beak

Name	Style	Intro	Gen	$	Note
Blue	90093	11/30/07	4	25	large
Bo	9706	12/30/03	4	11	
Bones	9377	6/24/00	4	11	
Bongo	9312	1/1/99	2, 3	11, 11	
Bonnet	94003	2/22/05	4,4	18, 11	Harrods UK, Ty Store
Bonsai	9494	6/30/03	4	11	
Booties	90007	6/30/04	4	11	
Bravo	9985	8/9/03	4	12	Trade Show
Brigitte	9435	12/27/01	4	11	
Britannia	9601	8/31/99	3	75	UK
Bronty	9353	1/4/00	4	15	
Brutus	90082	6/29/07	4	11	
Bubbles	9323	1/1/99	2, 3	12, 11	
Buckingham	9607	2/4/01	4	45	UK
Bunga Raya	9615	9/17/02	4	25	Malaysia
Bushy	9382	6/24/00	4	11	
Butch	9452	4/30/02	4	11	
Carnation	90008	6/30/04	4	11	
Cashew	9437	1/29/02	4	11	American Red Cross

Name	Style	Intro	Gen	$	Note
Cassie	9405	4/1/01	4	11	
Celebrate	9423	6/23/01	4	11	Trade Show/15th Anniversary
Centennial	none	9/14/03	4	75	New York Yankees
Champion	9501	4/4/02	4	12, 11	bears from 32 countries
Charmed	90067	12/29/06	4	11	
Charmer	9492	6/30/03	4	11	
Charming	90046	1/31/06	4	11	
Cheeks	9434	12/27/01	4	11	
Cheery	9456	5/31/02	4	11	
Chilly	9317	1/1/99	2, 3	15, 15	
Chinook	9605	7/30/02	4	18	Canada
Chip	9318	1/1/99	2, 3	11, 11	
Chocolate	9349	1/4/00	4	11	
Chops	9394	1/1/01	4	12	
Cinders	9443	3/1/02	4	11	
Classy	9458	6/28/02	4	11	
Clover	9477	12/27/02	4	11	
Clubby	9990	8/4/99	3	11	
Clubby II	9991	8/4/99	3	11	
Clubby III	9993	9/18/00	4	11	
Clubby IV	9994	9/24/01	4	11	
Clubby V	9995	9/16/02	4	11	5th Anniversary
Clubby VI	99000	12/1/04	4	12	BBOC
Colosso	9704	11/26/03	4	11	
Coolstina	90095	9/28/07	4	11	
Coolston	90094	9/28/07	4	11	
Congo	9361	1/4/00	4	11	
Coop	90072	1/31/07	4	11	
Coral	9381	6/24/00	4	11	
Coreana	9617	11/10/03	4	25	Asian-Pacific
Corkie	90047	1/31/06	4	11	

Cheeks

Clubby V

Name	Style	Intro	Gen	$	Note
Courage	9503	5/24/02	4	11	Ty Store
Cupid	9703	11/26/03	4	11	
Curly	9463	7/30/02	4	11	
Cutesy	90023	2/28/05	4	11	
DAD-e	9720	3/30/04	4	11	
Darling	9464	7/30/02	4	11	
Dearest	9448	3/1/02	4	11	
Delilah	90026	3/31/05	4	11	
Demure	90012	9/30/04	4	11	
Diddley	9462	6/28/02	4	12	
Diego	90091	1/2/08	4	20	large
Digger	9351	1/4/00	4, 4	12, 12	orange, ty-dye body
Diggs	90015	12/30/04	4	11	
Diggs	90016	12/30/04	4	25	large
Dippy	9716	1/30/04	4	11	
Divalectable	90068	7/31/06	4	11	
Dizzy	9450	4/1/02	4	11	

Name	Style	Intro	Gen	$	Note
Docks	90076	2/28/07	4	11	
Dora	90060	8/31/06	4	11	Ty Store
Dora	90090	1/2/08	4	20	large
Dotty	9364	1/4/00	4	11	
Dotty	9051	1/1/01	4	50	large
Dotty	9052	1/1/01	4	75	extra large
Dragon	9365	1/4/00	4	11	
Dublin	9711	12/30/03	4	15	
Ears	9388	1/1/01	4	12	
Ears	9046	1/1/01	4	45	large
Ears	9047	1/1/01	4	75	extra large
Eggbert	9442	12/27/01	4	45	
Eggs	9447	1/29/02	4	11	
Employee Bear	9373	6/24/00	4	12	
Empress	9495	6/30/03	4	11	
Erin	9309	1/1/99	2, 3	11, 11	
Eucalyptus	9363	1/4/00	4	11	
Fancy	9717	2/26/04	4	11	
Farley	90083	6/29/07	4	11	
Ferny	9613	9/17/02	4	45	New Zealand
Fetch	9338	8/31/99	3	30	
Filly	9708	12/30/03	4	11	
First Dog	90078	4/30/07	4	11	
Fitz	90027	3/31/05	4	11	
Fleece	9441	12/27/01	4	12	
Flip	9359	1/4/00	4	12	
Flippity	9358	1/4/00	4	11	
Flitter	9384	6/24/00	4	11	
Floppity	9390	1/1/01	4	12	
Floxy	90071	1/31/07	4	11	
Fraidy	9498	8/28/03	4	15	
Frankenteddy	94006	9/27/06	4	11	Ty Store

Fun

Garfield

Name	Style	Intro	Gen	$	Note
Frisbee	9455	5/31/02	4	20	$80 w/Wham-o hang tag
Frisco	9705	11/26/03	4	12	
Frolic	9484	2/28/03	4	11	
Fumbles	90021	2/28/05	4	11	
Fun	99001	10/2/06	4	11	BBOC
Fuzz	9328	4/1/99	3, 4	11, 12	
Fuzz	9040	1/4/00	4	45	large
Garfield	90020	1/31/05	4	11	Ty Store: sitting up
Garfield	90074	3/30/07	4	11	Ty Store: lying down
Garfield Season's Greetings	90063	9/29/06	4	11	
Germania	9603	2/4/00	4	14	Germany
Ghoul	90058	8/31/06	4	11	

Name	Style	Intro	Gen	$	Note
Ghoulianne	90059	8/31/06	4	11	
Gifts	90041	9/30/05	4	11	
Gift-wrapped	90062	9/29/06	4	11	
Giganto	9473	10/30/02	4	20	
GiGi	9700	9/30/03	4	11	
Glory	9410	5/1/01	4	11	USA
Gobbles	9333	8/31/99	3	11	tail attached/detached
Goochy	9362	1/4/00	4	11	
Grace	9389	1/1/01	4	12	
Groovy	9345	1/4/00	4	11	
Gussy	90070	12/29/06	4	11	Charlotte's Web
Halo	9337	8/31/99	3, 4	12, 12	
Halo II	9386	9/28/00	4	12	
Happy	9375	6/24/00	4	11	
Happy Birthday	9491	6/30/03	4	11	
Happy Birthday	90055	6/30/06	4, 4	11, 11	blue, green hat
Happy Birthday	90097	10/31/07	4	11	red hat
Haunt	9465	8/29/02	4	11	
Heartford	90014	11/30/04	4	11	
Herald	9496	7/31/03	4	11	
Herder	9487	4/30/03	4	11	
Hero	9449	4/1/02	4	11	
Hero 2004	90004	5/28/04	4	11	
Hippie	9357	1/4/00	4	11	
Hippie	9039	1/4/00	4, 4	75, 45	extra large, large
Hippity	9324	1/1/99	2, 3	11, 11	
Hocus	90038	8/31/05	4	11	
Hoofer	9472	10/30/02	4	14	
Hootie	90088	8/3/07	4	11	
Hope	9327	4/19/99	3, 4	11, 11	
Hopper	9438	12/27/01	4	11	
Hoppity	9439	12/27/01	4	13	

Groovy

Happy Birthday

Name	Style	Intro	Gen	$	Note
Hornsly	9407	4/1/01	4	11	
Huggy	9457	6/28/02	4	11	
Hug-hug	94004	1/10/06	4	11	
Humphrey	9307	9/30/98	1, 2, 3	12, 11, 11	
Ice Skates	6228	4/30/07	4	11	Canada
Inch	9331	6/26/99	3	11	
Independence	90055	4/30/07	4	11	red, blue, or white bow
India	9406	4/1/01	4	11	
Inky	9404	4/1/01	4	11	
It's A Boy	9479	12/27/02	4	11	
It's A Girl	9480	12/27/02	4	11	
Jabber	9326	4/16/99	3	11	
Jake	9304	9/30/98	1, 2, 3	11, 11, 11	

Name	Style	Intro	Gen	$	Note
John	90052	4/28/06	4	11	
Kicks	9343	1/4/00	4	11	
Kiki	90054	6/30/06	4	11	
Kirby	9702	9/30/03	4	11	
Kissable	90098	11/30/07	4	11	
KISS-e	9507	1/13/04	4	12	Ty Store
Kissme	9476	12/27/02	4	12	
Kiwiana	9619	11/10/03	4	25	Asian-Pacific
Knuckles	9460	6/28/02	4	14	
Koowee	96229	7/6/07	4	11	Astralia/New Zealand
Laughter	99001	10/1/06	4	12	BBOC
Lefty	9370	6/24/00	4	12	USA
Legs	9445	3/1/02	4	12	
Li Mei	90033	5/31/05	4	11	
Libearty	9371	6/24/00	4	12	USA
Libearty	9041	6/24/00	4	45	large
Libearty	9042	6/24/00	4	75	extra large
Liberty	9488	4/30/03	4	14	USA: red, white or blue face
Lips	9355	1/4/00	4	11	
Lizzy	9366	1/4/00	4	11	
Loosy	9428	10/1/01	4	11	
Lucky	9354	1/4/00	4	11	
Luke	9412	7/3/01	4	15	
Lullaby	9712	12/30/03	4	11	
M.C. Beanie	94005	1/20/06	4	11	Ty MBNA: black or brown nose
Magic	9466	8/29/02	4	11	
Maple	9600	8/31/99	3, 4	30, 30	Canada
Mattie	9481	12/27/02	4	12	
McWooly	90018	12/30/04	4	11	
Meekins	90045	12/30/05	4	11	

M.C. Beanie

Patrick Star

Name	Style	Intro	Gen	$	Note
Mellow	9411	7/3/01	4	12	
Millennium	9325	4/8/99	3	11	
Mom	90025	3/31/05	4	11	
Mooch	9416	7/31/01	4	25	
Mother	9718	2/26/04	4	11	
Mr.	9714	1/30/04	4	11	
Mrs.	9715	1/30/04	4	11	
Mugungwha	9611	9/17/02	4	25	Korea
Mum	9485	2/28/03	4	11	
My Mom	90073	2/28/07	4	11	
Mystic	9396	1/1/01	4	11	
Nanook	9350	1/4/00	4	25	
Neon	9417	7/31/01	4	11	
Nipponia	9606	5/1/02	4	30	Japan
Nutty	90089	8/31/07	4	11	
Oats	9392	1/1/01	4	12	

Name	Style	Intro	Gen	$	Note
Osito	9344	1/4/00	4	11	USA
Parfum	9707	12/30/03	4	12	
Patrick Star	90049	2/28/06	4	11	SpongeBob Squarepants
Patti	9320	1/1/99	2, 3	11, 11	
Peace	9335	8/31/99	3, 4	12, 12	dark original, pastel body
Peace	9037	1/4/00	4	45	large
Peace	9036	1/4/00	4	75	extra large
Peace	9035	1/4/00	4	150	jumbo
Peace Symbol	9709	12/30/03	4	12	
Peanut	9300	9/30/98	4	20	light blue body
Peanut	9300	9/30/98	1, 2, 3	20, 20, 20	royal blue body
Peking	9310	1/1/99	2, 3	12, 12	
Periwinkle	9415	7/3/01	4	11	
Pierre	9604	12/27/01	4	20	Canada
Pinchers	9424	7/31/01	4	12	
Pineapple Home	90035	2/28/05	4	11	SpongeBob Squarepants
Pinky	9316	1/1/99	2, 3	11, 11	
Ponder	90085	6/29/07	4	11	
Poofie	9461	6/28/02	4	11	
Pooky	90019	1/31/05	4	11	Garfield
Pooky	90042	9/30/05	4	11	Garfield: w/Santa hat
Poopsie	9444	12/27/01	4	11	
Poseidon	9490	4/30/03	4	15	
Pouch	9380	6/24/00	4	11	
Pounce	9436	3/1/02	4	11	
Prince	9401	1/1/01	4	11	
Princess	9329	4/23/99	3	12	
Pugsly	9413	7/3/01	4	25	
Pumkin'	9332	8/31/99	3	11	fruit/vegetable tag
Purr	9451	5/1/02	4	11	
Quackers	9302	9/30/98	3	175	no wings

Peace

Rover

Name	Style	Intro	Gen	$	Note
Quackers	9302	9/30/98	1, 2, 3	12, 12, 12	w/wings
Quivers	94001	9/27/04	4	12	
Radar	9422	9/3/01	4	12	
Rainbow	9367	1/4/00	4	11	
Ratzo	90039	8/31/05	4	11	
Red	90001	4/29/04	4	11	
Regal	9433	12/27/01	4	12	
Rescue	9502	5/24/02	4	14	Ty Store
Rex	9368	5/1/00	4	12	
Righty	9369	6/24/00	4	12	USA
Roam	9378	6/24/00	4	11	
Romance	9475	12/27/02	4	11	
Romeo & Juliet	90066	11/30/06	4	12	

Name	Style	Intro	Gen	$	Note
Rover	9305	9/30/98	1, 2, 3	12, 12, 12	
Roxie	90011	9/30/04	4	12	
Rufus	9393	1/1/01	4	15	
Sakura	9608	2/19/01	4	22	Japan
Sakura II	9610	9/17/02	4	22	Japan
Sam	90030	4/29/05	4	12	red, white or blue body
Sampson	9710	12/30/03	4	11	
Santa	9385	9/28/00	4	11	
SCARED-e	9497	8/28/03	4	20	
Schnitzel	9493	6/30/03	4	11	
Schweetheart	9330	6/26/99	3	15	
Schweetheart	9043	6/24/00	4	45	large
Schweetheart	9044	6/24/00	4	75	extra large
Schweetheart	9045	6/24/00	4	175	Jumbo
Scoop	90003	4/29/04	4	11	
Seal	9419	7/3/01	4	11	
Secret	94002	1/12/05	4	12	
Shamrock	9431	12/27/01	4	11	
Shamrock	9055	12/27/01	4	50	large
Shamrock	9056	12/27/01	4	11	extra large
Sherbet	9482	2/28/03	4, 4	15, 15	lt yellow, lt green
Sherbet	9486	5/29/03	4, 4	15, 15	lilac, pink
Shivers	90087	8/31/07	4	11	
Siam	9483	2/28/03	4	11	
Silver	9340	8/31/99	3	14	
Singabear	9620	11/10/03	4	25	Asian-Pacific
Sizzle	9432	12/27/01	4	11	
Slither	9339	8/31/99	3	12	
Smooch	9430	12/27/01	4	12	
Smoochy	9315	1/1/99	2, 3	12, 12	
Sneaky	9376	6/24/00	4	11	
Snort	9311	1/1/99	2, 3	11, 11	

Siam

Spangle

Name	Style	Intro	Gen	$	Note
Snowball	9429	10/1/01	4	12	
Snowboy	9342	8/31/99	3	12	
Soar	9489	5/29/03	4	15	USA
Spangle	9336	8/31/99	3, 4	14, 14	
Speckles	9500	1/10/02	4	12	Ty Store
Speedy	9352	1/4/00	4	12	
Spinner	9334	8/31/99	3	11	
SpongeBob	90048	2/28/06	4	11	
SpongeBob	90092	11/30/07	4	20	large
SpongeBob FrankenStein	90057	8/31/06	4	11	
SpongeBob's Pineapple Home	90035	2/28/05	4	12	
Spooky	9421	9/3/01	4	11	
Sport	90031	6/30/05	4	11	

Name	Style	Intro	Gen	$	Note
Spring	9478	12/27/02	4	11	
Spunky	9400	1/1/01	4	18	
Squealer	9313	1/1/99	2, 3	12, 12	
Star	90036	9/30/05	4, 4	12, 12	blue, gold star
Starlett	9459	6/28/02	4	12	
Steg	9383	6/24/00	4	12	
Stretch	9303	9/30/98	1, 2, 3	12, 12, 12	
Sunburst	90077	2/28/07	4	11	
Sundar	90034	5/31/05	4	11	
Sunny	9414	7/3/01	4	12	
Sweetest	94000	9/15/04	4	12	Ty Store
Swinger	90086	7/31/07	4	11	
Swoop	9391	1/1/01	4	11	
Tangerine	9418	9/3/01	4, 4	12, 12	plush fabric, terry cloth
Teddy	9306	9/30/98	1, 2, 3	11, 11, 11	cranberry body
Teddy	9372	6/24/00	4	11	teal body
The Beginning	9399	1/1/01	4	11	
The Cardinal	9395	1/1/01	4	11	
Thomas	90050	4/28/06	4	11	
Thunderbolt	90065	11/30/06	4	11	
Top Dog	90024	3/31/05	4	12	
Tracker	9319	1/1/99	2, 3	20, 20	
Tradee	9504	4/30/02	4	12	Ty Store
Tradition	none	9/25/05	4	75	New York Yankees
Trotter	9446	12/27/01	4	30	
True	96223	4/28/06	4	11	
Trumpet	9403	4/1/01	4	15	
Tumba	90080	5/31/07	4	11	
Tumba	90081	5/31/07	4	30	large
Twigs	9308	9/30/98	1, 2	110, 110	
Twitch	90028	4/29/05	4	20	
Ty 2K	9346	1/4/00	4	12	

Sunny

Teddy

Name	Style	Intro	Gen	$	Note
Unity	9609	10/1/01	4	18	Europe
USA	9453	4/30/02	4	11	USA
Valentina	9397	1/1/01	4	11	
Valentina	9048	1/1/01	4	45	large
Valentina	9049	1/1/01	4	75	extra large
Valentina	9050	1/1/01	4	175	jumbo
Valentino	9347	1/4/00	4	11	
Valor	90005	5/28/04	4	12	
Vanda	9614	9/17/02	4	25	Singapore
Veggies	90044	12/30/05	4	11	
Waddle	9314	1/1/99	2, 3	11, 11	
Wallace	9387	9/28/00	4	11	
Wattlie	9612	9/17/02	4	25	Australia
Webley	90075	3/30/07	4	11	

Ty 2K

Valentino

Name	Style	Intro	Gen	$	Note
Weenie	9356	1/4/00	4	17	
White	90001	4/29/04	4	11	
White Tiger	9374	6/24/00	4	17	
Whittle	90022	2/28/05	4	11	
Wilbur	90069	12/29/06	4	11	Charlotte's Web
Wirabear	9621	11/10/03	4	25	AP: Malaysia
Woody	9499	8/28/03	4	12	
World Class	none	8/8/04	4	75	New York Yankees
Wrinkles	9440	3/1/02	4	11	
Y Ddraig Goch	96224	8/15/06	4	11	UK
Yankees Pride	none	10/1/06	4	75	New York Yankees
Yapper	90029	4/29/05	4	11	
Zeus	90006	6/30/04	4	12	
Zip	9360	1/4/00	4	12	

Ty Beanie Kids

Top Row: Calypso, Buzz, Ginger, Specs
Bottom Row: Precious, Blondie, Cutie

Nine Beanie Kids made their debut in 2000 as the first line of dolls. By the end of 2003, thc only current Beanie Kid was BABE-e 2003. The 10" Beanie Kids feature soft bodies and either curly or rather wild straight hair that can be arranged in different hairstyles. They feature details such as sewn belly buttons and hand-painted crystal eyes. Ty Gear is a line of clothing especially designed for them.

BABE-e

Buzz

Name	Style	Intro	Gen	$	Note
Angel	0001	1/8/00	1, 2	10, 8	velcro, elastic fastener
BABE-e	0024	12/16/02	2	10	Ty Store
Baby 2002	0022	11/30/01	2	10	
Blondie	0017	1/1/01	2	8	
Boomer	0007	1/8/00	1, 2	8, 8	
Buzz	0010	6/24/00	2	8	
Calypso	0011	6/24/00	2	8	
Chipper	0008	1/8/00	1, 2	8, 8	
Cookie	0013	6/24/00	2	8	
Curly	0004	1/8/00	1, 2	10, 8	velcro, elastic fastener
Cutie	0005	1/8/00	1, 2	10, 8	velcro, elastic fastener
Dumplin'	0023	4/1/02	2	10	

Cookie

Curly

Name	Style	Intro	Gen	$	Note
Ginger	0003	1/8/00	1, 2	10, 8	velcro, elastic fastener
Jammer	0016	1/1/00	2	8	
Luvie	0014	1/1/00	2	9	
Noelle	0020	10/1/01	2	12	
Precious	0002	1/8/00	1, 2	18, 8	velcro, elastic fastener
Princess	0012	6/24/00	2	8	
Rascal	0006	1/8/00	1, 2	8, 8	
Shenanigan	0015	1/1/01	2	8	
Specs	0018	1/1/01	2	10	
Sugar	0019	11/30/01	2	10	
Sweetie	0021	11/30/01	2	10	
Tumbles	0009	1/8/00	1, 2	8, 8	

Jammer

Luvie

Shenanigan

Sugar

Ty Bow Wow Beanies

Snort, Pink Stripe, Weenie, Bones

This collection was made especially for dogs, so each one is constructed from sturdy fabric to make them chewable. Some of them make crinkle noises and squeak. Bones are featured in a variety of fabric prints and colored trims, and there are also characters similar to the regular Beanie Babies like Quackers, Lizzy, and Nuts. Three comical Garfields™ are included. All Bow Wow Beanies have single (nonfolding) 1st Generation hang tags.

Name	Style	Bday	$
Bat	43022	8/31/07	6
Blue Seal	43027	9/28/07	6
Bones	43007	3/31/06	6
Camouflage	43300	3/31/06	6
Camouflage (small)	43301	3/31/06	5
Candy Cane Bone	43301	3/31/06	5
Chillin'	43016	9/29/06	5
Chocolate	43017	9/29/06	5
Cow Print	43314	12/29/06	6
Duck	43030	10/31/07	6
Foxy	43028	2/28/07	5
Garfield - Bite Me!	43019	2/28/07	6
Garfield - Cats Rule!	43020	2/28/07	6
Garfield - Play Nice!	43021	2/28/07	6
Green Snowflake	43310	9/29/06	5
Halloween	43308	8/31/06	5
Halloween Bones	43023	8/31/07	6
Hearts	43307	3/31/06	6
Inky	43004	3/31/06	6
Legs	43000	3/31/06	5
Leopard Print	43313	12/29/06	6
Lil' Bones	43008	3/31/06	5
Lil' Legs	43001	3/31/06	5
Lizzy	43003	3/31/06	6
Nuts	43005	3/31/06	6
Palm Trees	43305	3/31/06	6
Patti	43006	3/31/06	6
Paw Prints	43304	3/31/06	6
Pink 60's Print	43312	12/29/06	6
Pink Stripe	43302	3/31/06	6
Pink Stripe (small)	43303	3/31/06	5
Prickles	43011	3/31/06	6

Garfield - Cats Rule, Legs

Patti

Name	Style	Bday	$
Pumpkin	43014	8/31/06	5
Quackers	43010	3/31/06	6
Red Snowflake	43309	9/29/06	5
Red White And Blue Stars	43306	3/31/06	6
Snort	43012	3/31/06	6
Snowflake Bone	43024	9/28/07	6
Springtime Bear	43018	1/31/07	6
Stinky	43013	3/31/06	6
Stripe	43011	9/29/06	5
Tan Dog	43029	10/31/07	6
Trap	43002	3/31/06	6
Weenie	43009	3/31/06	6
Zero	43015	9/29/06	5

Top Row: Hightops, Mercury, Opal
Bottom Row: Glamour, Teddybearsary, Romeo, Piston

Ty Classic

The Ty Plush line, later known as Classic, was introduced in 1985 as the first of all of the Ty lines. Originally it just featured cats and dogs, but the line was expanded to include a wide variety of animals made from different furs and in different poses. The sizes range from 9" to 36", and many of them have numerous variations. The classic line continues to thrive.

Al E Kat

Allioop

Name	Style	Intro	Gen	$
1991 Collectible Bear	5500	1991	2	400
1992 Collectible Bear	5500	1992	2	350
1997 Holiday Teddy	5700	1997	3	20
Ace	2027	1998	3	40
Al E Kat	1111	1989, 1992	1, 2	300, 150
Al E Kat	1111	1996	3	30
Al E Kat	1111	1998	1	400
Al E Kat	1112	1996, 1998	3, 1	35, 300
Al E Kat	1112	1992	2	150
Alacazam	80110	8/31/05	4	11
Alfalfa	8103	12/30/03	4	13
Allioop	1131	2001	4	20
Alpine	50004	10/29/04	4	20
Angel	1001	1988	1, 2, 3	300, 100, 30
Angel	10015	4/28/06	4	12
Angel	1001H	1985	1, 2	500, 250
Angel	1001H	1985	1, 2	600, 300

Name	Style	Intro	Gen	$
Angel	1001H	1985	1, 2	700, 350
Angel	1122	1988	3	30
Angelina	5051	9/30/02	4	15
Angora	1001	1986	1	1,500
Angora	8004	1985	2, 3	20, 35
Angora	8005	1991	1, 2	100, 100
Apricot	10002	6/30/04	4	13
Arctic	7419	1995	3	20
Arnold	6002	1990	1	125
Ashes	2018	1992	3	15
Aubrey	50026	12/29/06	4	12
Auburn	5119	7/3/01	4	20
Aurora	5103	1996	3	25
Baby Angora	1002	1986	1	1,500
Baby Auburn	5118	7/3/01	4	13
Baby Bijan	1006	1986	1	2,500
Baby Buddy	5011	1992	2	200
Baby Butterball	2006	1986	1	1,500
Baby Camper	5123	12/27/02	4	1,600
Baby Cinnamon	5105	1996	3	25
Baby Clover	8023	1993	2	100
Baby Curly	5017	1993	2, 3	65, 20
Baby Curly	5018	Unknown	None	20
Baby Curly	5018	1993	3	15
Baby Curly	5018	2000	4	15
Baby Curly	5018	2000	4	15
Baby Curly	5018	2001	4	15
Baby Curly	5018	1998	3	15
Baby Curly	8024	1993	2, 3	50, 20
Baby Curly	8025	1993	2, 3	50, 20
Baby George	70010	1/31/06	4	12
Baby George	7300	1996	3	20

Aubrey

Baby Iceberg

Name	Style	Intro	Gen	$
Baby Ginger	5108	1997	3	22
Baby Goldilocks	5057	12/30/03	4	12
Baby Iceberg	5040	2003	4	13
Baby Iceberg	5040	2001	4	11
Baby Iceberg	5055	2004	4	11
Baby Jasmine	1004	1986	1	2,000
Baby Kasha	1008	1986	1	2,000
Baby Kimchi	2004	1986	1	2,000
Baby Li-Li	5115	7/3/01	4	14
Baby Lovie	8019	1992	2	90
Baby Lovie	8020	1993	2	70
Baby Oscar	2008	1986	1	1,500
Baby Patches	2030	1999	3	40
Baby Paws	5004	6/30/03	4	12
Baby Paws	5110	1997	3	22
Baby Paws	5111	1997	3	22

Name	Style	Intro	Gen	$
Baby Paws	5112	1998	3	25
Baby Petunia	8021	1993, 1994	2, 3	75, 25
Baby PJ	5016	1993	2, 3	30, 20
Baby PJ	5100	1994	2	125
Baby Pokey	8022	1996	3	25
Baby Powder	5109	1997	3	24
Baby Rumbles	7411	12/27/02	4	20
Baby Schnapps	3001	1996	1	2,000
Baby Smokey	8023	1996	3	20
Baby Snowball	2002	1986	1	1,000
Baby Sparky	2012	1992, 1994	2, 3	70, 40
Baby Spice	5104	1996	3	20
Baby Xio Lin	5135	2/26/04	4	12
Bag O' Treats	80123	8/31/06	4	12
Bailey	5502	1997	3	30
Bamboo	5033	2000	4	25
Bamboo	5106	1996	3	25
Bamboo	5113	1998	3	21
Bandit	1119	1990	1	200
Bandit	8009	1992	2, 3	75, 25
Bangles	10003	11/30/04	4	18
Barney	2003	1990	1, 2	175, 50
Baron	5200	1995	2, 3	30, 25
Bashful	20004	1/3/05	4	20
Bayou	7445	12/31/03	4	12
Beanie Bear	5000	1988	1, 2	300, 150
Beanie Bear	5100	1991	2	300
Beanie Bunny	8000	1989	1, 2	250, 175
Beanie Bunny	8001	1991	2	12
Beans	80121	5/30/06	4	12
Bearnaise	50033	6/29/07	4	15
Bearnard	5300	6/30/04	4	12

Bamboo

Bayou

Name	Style	Intro	Gen	$
Beasley	2050	6/28/02	4	12
Beaut	7443	6/30/05	4	12
Belevedere	5031	2000	4	18
Bengal	7423	1995, 1998	2, 3	30, 20
Bengal	7423	1998	3	15
Big Beanie Bear	5011	1990	1	350
Big Beanie Bunny	8011	1991	2	200
Big Beanie Bunny	8011	1990	1	300
Big Beanie Bunny	8012	1991	2	200
Big George	7302	1990	4	200, 75, 60
Big Jake	7002C	1989	1	200
Big Jake	7200	1990	1	200
Big Jake	7201	1990	1	200
Big Jake	7202	1990	1	200
Big Pudgy	9006	1994	2, 3	70, 50
Big Shaggy	9015	1992	2	125
Bijan	1005	1986	1	1,500
Billings	80124	1/31/07	4	10
Billingsly	80115	1/1/06	4	12
Binks	5127	12/27/02	4	12
Biscuit	2026	1987	3	30
Bixie	20047	4/30/07	4	10
Blackie	5003	1998	1	200
Blossom	1134	8/31/00	4	20
Blossom	8013	1996	3	30
Blueberry	5312	1999	4	13
Bluesy	75003	6/30/05	4	10
Blushed	70017	11/30/06	4	14
Blushing	5132	11/26/03	4	16
Bo	2009	1994	2, 3	100, 40
Boggs	20022	1/1/06	4	12
Bojangles	5126	12/27/02	4	14

Billings

Bumpkin

Name	Style	Intro	Gen	$
Boone	20031	6/30/06	4	12
Boots	1132	1998	4	28
Boudreaux	50012	1/1/06	4	12
Bows	8030	1998	3	20
Bramble	80118	1/1/06	4	13
Brinksie	20024	1/1/06	4	12
Bristol	50002	6/30/05	4	14
Broderick	5032	2000	4	16
Brodie	20023	1/1/06	4	12
Brooke	70009	5/31/05	4	15
Brownie	5100	1996	2, 3	35, 20
Buckshot	2009	1992	2	180
Buckshot	70005	2/28/05	4	14
Buddy	5007	6/12/05	1, 2	300, 125
Buddy	5019	1993	2, 3	60, 30
Bumpkin	50037	8/31/07	4	12

Name	Style	Intro	Gen	$
Buster	2005	1990	1, 2	350, 100
Butterball	2005	1986	1	1,500
Butterbeary	5311	1999	3	30
Buttercup	8012	1996	3	35
Buttermilk	80122	5/30/06	4	10
Buttons	8031	1998	3	18
Caboodle	10014	10/31/05	4	16
Caesar	7440	6/30/05	4	12
Calhoun	2063	6/30/05	4	16
Cameo	1144	12/27/02	4	11
Camper	5122	12/27/02	4	20
Candy	8011	1996	3	40
Caressa	50009	11/30/05	4	18
Carley	1135	1/1/05	4	20
Carroty	50029	1/31/07	4	12
Cartwheels	670006	2/28/05	4	16
Carver	50020	8/31/06	4	10
Carvington	80106	8/31/05	4	10
Cashmere	8030	1/1/01	4	13
Cashmere	8032	12/28/01	4	12
Cassidy	10010	6/30/05	4	10
Catalina	100118	6/30/06	4	12
Catskills	10023	12/29/06	4	12
Caviar	10001	6/30/04	4	20
Celeste	50028	12/29/06	4	12
Cha Cha	7005	1998	3	24
Champagne	10004	2/28/05	4	30
Charisse	50017	6/30/05	4	12
Charlie	2001	1998	1	225
Charlie	2001, 2005	1990, 1996	1, 3	225, 35
Charlie	2005	1994	2, 3	75, 40
Chestnut	8022	1993	2	125

Carroty

Catskills

Name	Style	Intro	Gen	$
Chestnuts	70015	9/29/06	4	13
Chewey	2067	12/31/03	4	15
Chica	1147	6/30/05	4	12
Chi-Chi	1114	1989, 1990	1, 2	275, 100
Chi-Chi	7414	1991	2	75
Chips	20006	1/31/05	4	13
Chips	2025	1997	3	25
Chuckles	7303	1997	3	30
Churchhill	2017	1996	3	25
Cinders	2008	1994, 1995	2, 3	60, 35
Cinnamon	5004	1989	1	200
Cinnamon	5012	1996	3	35
Clover	8007	1991, 1994	2, 2	175, 70
Clover	8007	1991	2, 3	125, 40
Coal	1119	1997	3	32
Cobble	10029	4/30/07	4	10

Name	Style	Intro	Gen	$
Cobbler	10031	6/29/07	4	12
Cocoa	5107	1997	3	22
Cocoa	57003	None	4	15
Cody	2051	6/28/02	4	20
Colonel	20027	6/30/06	4	10
Cooper	80109	12/30/04	4	10
Corky	2023	1996	3	20
Cotton	8002	1996	3	30
Cradles	53006	2/28/06	4	15
Crockett	5129	6/30/03	4	12
Crush	20020	11/30/05	4	11
Crystal	1120	1997	3	35
Curly	5302	2000	4	20
Curly	5200	1991	2	100
Curly	5301	1991	2	125
Curly	5302	1993, 2000	2, 4	50, 20
Curly	5302	1998, 2001	3, 4	30, 20
Curly Bunny	8017	1992	4	25
Curly Bunny	8018	1992	4	25
Curly Bunny	8018	1998	2, 3	75, 35
Curly Bunny	8017	2001	2, 3	50, 35
Curly Bunny	8017	1998	2, 3	50, 20
Cuzzy	5203	1996	3	40
Cyrano	27003	1/4/07	4	11
Cyrano	27003	1/4/07	4	11
Daisy	20054	10/31/07	4	12
Dakota	7418	1995, 1998	3, 3	25, 20
Dancer	20002	9/30/04	4	15
Dash	7432	2000	4	16
Destiny	10009	6/30/05	4	10
Dewdrops	50034	6/29/07	4	12
Diesel	70025	6/29/07	4	20

Cradles

Daisy

Name	Style	Intro	Gen	$
Digby	56008	11/4/06	4	30
Digits	7444	12/31/03	4	20
Dinger	20048	5/31/07	4	10
Diploma	20029	3/31/06	4	12
Dipper	70022	1/31/07	4	12
Disco	2059	5/29/03	4	16
Divine	5045	7/3/01	4	14
Dodges	20017	6/30/05	4	16
Domino	8006	1991	2	15
Dopey	2022	1996	3	30
Dot	7433	2000	4	15
Dreamland	80129	6/29/07	4	12
Droopy	2009	1996	3	35
Duff	200049	6/29/07	4	10

Name	Style	Intro	Gen	$
Dumpling	5022	1996	3	35
Dumpling	5023	1996	3	35
Duster	2031	2000	3	30
Dustin	20003	6/30/04	4	20
Eggsworth	80117	1/1/06	4	15
Eleanor	5500	1996	3	35
Elmer	1116	1989, 1990	1, 1	200, 200
Elmer	7416	1994	2, 3	70, 30
Elmer	7416	1991	2	100
Elvis	2010	1995	2, 3	50, 25
Eureka	50027	12/29/06	4	12
Faith	5600	1996	3	22
Faithful	50018	6/30/06	4	10
Fargo	50021	9/29/06	4	15
Fenwick Holiday Teddy	56003	10/18/05	4	15
Fiddle	20025	1/31/06	4	12
Fiddles	10028	3/30/07	4	10
Fido	2019	1996	3	25
Fielding	80136	1/2/08	4	12
Flags	50015	4/28/06	4	12
Flecks	5036	8/31/00	4	11
Fletcher	50005	5/31/05	4	18
Flippers	7403	12/27/02	4	12
Flopper	2037	8/31/00	4	25
Flopster	8035	12/28/01	4	16
Fluff	2053	Summer 2003	4	15
Fluff	2053	8/29/02	4	13
Fluff	2053	Holiday 2003	4	15
Fluff	2053	Valentine 2004	4	15
Fluffy	1002	1996	3	35
Foofie	20010	12/30/04	4	12
Forest	5048	6/28/02	3	11

Eureka

Fielding

Name	Style	Intro	Gen	$
Forest	5114	1998	4	25
Freddie	1117	1989	1	200
Freddie	1117	1990	1	200
Freddie	8010	1991	2	75
Freddie	8010	1992	2, 3	50, 25
Fresco	53001	12/30/04	4	15
Frisky	1007	1996	3	70
Fritz	2002	1988, 1990	1, 1	200, 200
Fullhouse	57004	2007	4	10
Fuzzy	5204	1996	3	40
Galaxy	8102	12/31/03	4	15
Garfield & Pooky	10030	5/31/07	4	15
Garland	5053	9/30/03	4	13
George	7301	1990	1, 2, 3	150, 50, 35
Ginger	1007	1988	1	200
Ginger	1007H	1985	1, 2	2000, 1000

Glamour

Name	Style	Intro	Gen	$
Ginger	1007H	1985	1	1,000
Ginger	5306	1997	3	70
Glamour	1145	5/29/03	4	10
Glitz	1146	5/30/03	4	18
Gloria	5052	9/30/03	4	15
Godzilla	5614	11/1/01	4, 4	30, 20
Goldilocks	5308	12/31/03	4	20
Goldwyn	20042	12/29/06	4	10
Gourdin	80104	8/30/04	4	10
Grad	20046	3/30/07	4	12
Granola	5131	6/30/05	4	14
Griddles	5133	12/31/03	4	12
Grizzles	50013	1/31/06	4	10
Growl	7435	12/28/01	4	18
Gumdrop	5043	1/1/01	4	17
Hareston	80111	12/30/04	4	10

Hightops

Hucklebeary

Name	Style	Intro	Gen	$
Harewood	80126	1/31/07	4	18
Harris	1115	1989, 1990	1,1	400, 400
Harris	7415	1991	2, 3	60, 40
Hatcher	80116	1/1/06	4	20
Hickory	50030	5/31/07	4	12
Hightops	7442	6/30/05	4	12
Hightops (large)	70016	10/31/06	4	35
Honey	2001	1995	3	35
Honey	5004	1991	2	80
Hooters	8016	1992	2	125
Hope	5601	1996	3	21
Hucklebeary	57005	10/25/07		
Hudson	50023	10/31/06	4	13
Hugston	27002	1/26/06	4	13
Hutch	20005	6/30/04	4	12
Iceberg	5041	1/1/01	4	16

Name	Style	Intro	Gen	$
Iceberg	5041	2003	4	18
Iceberg	5056	9/30/03	4	16
Icicle	50008	9/30/05	4	12
Isis	1143	12/27/02	4	10
Jake	7001A	1989	1	250
Jake	7100	1992	2	75
Jake	7100	1990	1	250
Jake	7101	1992	2	75
Jake	7101	1990	1	250
Jake	7102	1990	1	250
Jake	7434	2000	4	18
Jasmine	1003	1986	1	200
Java	5049	6/28/02	4	14
Jax	20041	11/30/06	4	10
Jazzy	75001	6/30/05	4	11
Jeeves	5038	8/31/00	4	12
Jenkins	2041	7/3/01	4	15
Jersey (black)	8026	1997	3	40
Jersey (brown)	8026	1997	3	40
Jeweled	10022	12/29/06	4	10
Jonah	7404	12/27/02	4	12
Josh	7101	1994	2, 3	75, 50
Jumbles	10005	1/31/05	4	20
Jumbo George	9008	1991	2, 3	100, 75
Jumbo PJ	9016	1994	2	175
Jumbo PJ	9020	1992	2, 3	100, 60
Jumbo Pumpkin	9017	1995	3	75
Jumbo Rumples	9016	1995	3	75
Jumbo Shaggington	9101	7/3/01	4	40
Jumbo Shaggy	9016	1992	2	85
Jumbo Shaggy	9017	1992	2	85
Jumbo Shaggy	9026	1993	2	75

Jax

Jeweled

Name	Style	Intro	Gen	$
Kasey	5006	1989	2	100
Kasey	5006	1990	2	100
Kasha	1007	1986	1	2,500
Kimchi	2003	1986	1	2,500
King Ghidorah	5615	11/1/01	4	30
Kingly	7435	12/28/01	4	16
Kissed	80120	5/30/06	4	12
Kissycat	10013	11/30/05	4	11
Kit	10024	1/31/07	4	12
Kitty	1141	6/28/02	4	15
Kivu	7438	6/28/02	4	20
Kodi	20011	9/30/04	4	30
Laces	20016	5/31/05	4	16
Lacey	5121	6/28/02	4	12
Lacey	5121	Summer 2003	4	14
Lagoon	5046	12/28/01	4	16

Name	Style	Intro	Gen	$
Large Curly	9019	2000	4	25
Large Curly	9019	1998	2, 3	60, 40
Large Curly	9003	1994	2, 3	60, 40
Large Curly	9007	1996	3	40
Large Curly	9018	1992	2, 3	60, 40
Large Curly	9019	1992	2, 3	60, 40
Large Curly	9019	2000, 2001	4, 4	25, 25
Large Curly	9019	Fall 1988	4	25
Large Ginger	9027	1997	3	40
Large Harewood	80127	1/31/07	4	30
Large Honey	9021	1992	2	75
Large Li-Li	9010	7/3/01	4	50
Large McGee	9005	1992	2, 3	65, 40
Large Moonbeam	9009	1995	3	35
Large Paws	9004	6/30/03	4	26
Large Paws	9029	1997	3	40
Large Paws	9030	1997	3	40
Large Paws	9031	1998	3	40
Large Petunia	9003	1992	2	100
Large Ping Pong	9010	1992	2	100
Large Pinstripe	70012	1/1/06	4	40
Large PJ	9012	1992	2	80
Large PJ	9012	1993	2, 3	70, 40
Large PJ	9014	1994	2	100
Large Powder	9028	1997	3	35
Large Pumpkin	9015	1995	3	40
Large Rumples	9000	1995	3	50
Large Rumples	9002	1995	3	50
Large Rusty	9011	1994	2, 3	100, 50
Large Scruffy	9000	1992	2	100
Large Scruffy	9008	1992	2	100
Large Scruffy	9011	1992	2	100

Lilacbeary

Lovely

Name	Style	Intro	Gen	$
Large Scruffy	9013	1992	2	100
Large Shaggington	9013	7/3/01	4	28
Large Shaggy	9014	1993	2	100
Large Shaggy	9015	1992	2	100
Large Shaggy	9025	1992	2, 3	100, 50
Large Snowball	9009	1992	2	100
Large Sparkey	9002	1992	2	100
Lazy	5008	1995	3	40
Leo	7427	1997	3	45
Leonard	56005	12/1/05	4	10
Lexie	10008	6/30/05	4	10
Licorice	1009	1988	1, 2, 3	200, 100, 50
Licorice	1125	1998	3	35
Lilac	5128	12/31/03	4	10
Lilacbeary	5314	2000	4	13
Li-Li	5116	7/3/01	4	20

Name	Style	Intro	Gen	$
Lillie	8004	1990	1	200
Lilypad	74004	12/30/04	4	12
Lovely	80133	11/30/07	4	12
Lovie	8001	1988	1	200
Lovie	8004	1991	2	75
Lovie	8019	1993	2, 3	50, 35
Lovie	8027	1998	3	15
Lyric	10019	6/30/06	4	20
MacDougal	2048	12/28/01	4	12
Magee	5027	1988	3	18
Maggie	1115	1996	3	40
Maggie	111	1992	2, 3	50, 35
Magilicuddy	50010	1/1/06	4	15
Mandaarin	5201	1996	3	30
Mango	7100	1995	3	35
Mango	7102	1995	3	35
Max	2008	1991	2	125
Max	2036	8/31/00	4	15
Max	3001	1989, 1990	1, 1	300, 300
McGee	5001	1991	2, 3	60, 30
McGee	5001	1988	1	200
Meadow	8037	12/28/01	4	11
Melville	70003	10/29/04	4	10
Melvin	7413	12/27/02	4	10
Memphis	2049	12/28/01	4	18
Meows	10012	11/30/05	4	10
Mercury	2060	6/30/05	4	18
Merribear	57002	10/31/06	4	12
Merry	50003	9/30/04	4	10
Midnight	5009	1990	1	200
Midnight	5009	1991, 1993	2	100
Midnight	5101	1996	3	40

Meadow

Mercury

Name	Style	Intro	Gen	$
Mischief	7000	1990	1, 2	200, 100
Mischief	7001	1990	1, 2	200, 200
Mischief	70008	1989	1	250
Mischief	7002	1990	1, 2	200, 100
Mischief	7414	1996	3	40
Misty	7400	1991	2	125
Misty	7400	1993	2, 3	175, 45
Misty	7431	1998	3	25
Mitsy	20043	12/29/06	4	10
Mittens	1118	1993	2	100
Mittens	1117	6/15/05	2, 3	100, 30
Molasses	5125	12/27/02	4	16
Moonbeam	5009	1995	3	30
Moondust	56004	11/4/05	4	12
Moonstruck	10020	8/31/06	4	12

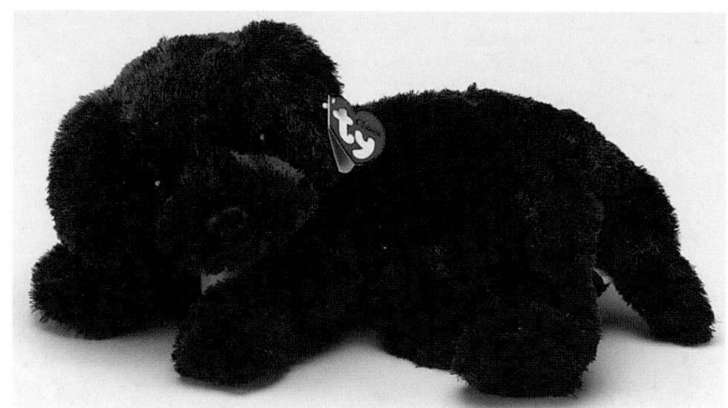

Nuzzle

Name	Style	Intro	Gen	$
Mootina	80000	9/30/04	4	16
Moppet	20036	7/31/06	4	10
Mortimer	7417	1996	3	35
Mothra	5616	12/1/01	4	60
Mr. Flurries	80112	9/30/05	4	15
Muffet	10027	3/30/07	4	15
Muffin	2020	1996	3	26
Mugsy	2052	6/28/02	4	15
Musher	2061	6/30/05	4	14
Mystery	1127	2000	4	15
Nibbles (brown)	8000	1994	3	20
Nibbles (white)	8001	1995	3	20
Nippey	2055	12/27/02	4	12
Nipsey	2057	12/27/02	4	20
Nutmeg	5013	1996	3	35
Nuzzle	2042	7/3/01	4	12

Opal

Piston

Name	Style	Intro	Gen	$
O' Malley	1140	6/28/02	4	14
Oasis	50000	6/30/04	4	10
Omelet	8014	9/30/03	4	13
Onyx	1136	1/1/01	4	25
Opal	80105	11/30/04	4	25
Opal	8101	6/30/03	4	15
Orchard	80125	1/31/07	4	12
Oreo	5005	1994	2, 3	100, 40
Oreo	5010	1990	1, 2	200, 100
Oscar	2007	1986	1	1,500
Otto	7417	1993	2	150
Outback	70023	6/29/07	4	10
Papa PJ	9021	1997	3	90
Papa Pumpkin	9023	1995	3	95
Papa Rumples	9022	1995	2, 3	250, 100
Papa Shaggy	9022	1991	2	300

Name	Style	Intro	Gen	$
Papa Shaggy	9024	1994	2, 3	300, 100
Patches	1114	1991	3	45
Patches	2003	1996	3	35
Patter	80113	11/30/05	4	10
Patti	1118	1989	1	200
Paws Black	5025	1997	3	35
Paws Maple	5301	6/30/03	4	20
Paws Sable	5024	1997	3	35
Paws White	5026	1998	3	35
Peaches	10016	4/28/06	4	20
Peaches	1003	1988	1, 2	200, 100
Peaches	1003H	1988	1, 2	1500, 500
Peachy	1137	7/3/01	4	30
Pearl	1133	8/31/00	4	16
Pecos	70021	1/31/07	4	10
Peepers	8015	1992	2	100
Penny	5039	8/31/00	4	12
Pepper	2024	1997	3	30
Perkins	2034	2000	4	20
Peter	8002	1989	1, 2	200, 100
Peter	8002	1996	3	35
Peter	8020	2000	4	20
Petunia	6001	1989	1	200
Petunia	8008	1992, 1993	2, 2	100, 100
Petunia	8008	1994	2, 3	100, 50
Pierre	2004	1995	3	20
Ping Pong	5005	1989	1	200
Pinstripes	70011	1/1/06	4	10
Pinwheel	50019	6/30/06	4	12
Piston	7441	6/30/05	4	12
Pitter	80114	11/30/05	4	10
PJ	5200	1994	2	100

Purplebeary

Pups-N-Kisses

Name	Style	Intro	Gen	$
PJ	5400	1991	2	100
PJ	5400	1993	2, 3	50, 35
PJ	5400	1991	2	100
Pokey	8015	1996	3	35
Porridge	5054	9/30/03	4	15
Powder	5607	1997	3	35
Prayer Bear	5600	1992	2	75
Prayer Bear	5601	1992	2	75
Presents	20019	9/30/05	4	11
Presto	80107	12/30/04	4	10
Prissy	1128	2000	4	18
Pudgy	5006	1994	2, 3	75, 30
Puffy	1003	1996	3	30
Pumpkin	5304	1995	3	35
Pups-N-Kisses	20055	11/30/07	4	12
Purplebeary	5313	1999	3	30
Purrecious	1142	11/27/02	4, 4	20, 18

Name	Style	Intro	Gen	$
Quackie	8033	1/1/01	4	11
Quake	70019	12/29/06	4	12
Rabble	20018	6/30/05	4	13
Rags	2035	1992	4	20
Rags	5102	6/14/05	2, 3	40, 28
Raindrops	50035	6/29/07	4	10
Raj	70041	6/30/06	4	20
Rascal	7001	1994	2, 3	75, 30
Razzatazz	5034	2000	4	18
Razzmatazz	5035	2000	4	18
Rebel	2058	5/26/04	4	15
Regent	70013	6/30/06	4	12
Rescue	2040	1/1/01	4	16
Ripples	2066	12/31/03	4	28
Rocker	75002	6/30/05	4	10
Roller	75004	6/30/05	4	10
Romancer	70018	11/30/06	4	15
Romantic	50042	11/30/07	4	12
Romeo	5310	1998, 1999	3, 3	30, 30
Romeo	5310	1998	3	30
Romper	2038	1/1/05	4	11
Roscoe	20050	6/29/07	4	10
Rosette	5120	1/1/01	4	15
Rosie	8003	1990	1, 2	300, 80
Rougue	5044	1/1/01	4	15
Ruffles	5014	1995	3	20
Rufus	5015	1993	2, 3	75, 35
Rumbles	7412	12/27/02	3	25
Rumples	5002	1995	3	40
Rumples	5003	1995	4	40
Rusty	2011	1992	2, 3	75, 35
Sahara	7421	1998	3	25

Romantic

Scoundrel

Name	Style	Intro	Gen	$
Sahara	7421	1995, 1996	2, 3	70, 25
Saint	5120	6/30/05	4	15
Sam	5010	1995	3	35
Sandy	20015	2/28/05	4	18
Sarge	2003	1994	2, 3	75, 40
Schnapps	3000	1986	1	2,000
Schultzie	2068	12/31/03	4	11
Scooter	2033	2000	4	20
Scoundrel	20037	7/31/06	4	12
Scrapper	2056	12/27/02	4	12
Scraps	2047	12/28/01	4	20
Scratch	117	1996	3	30
Screech	116	1995	2, 3	70, 35
Scruffy	2000	1992, 1993	2, 2	75, 75
Scruffy	2001	1991	2	75

Name	Style	Intro	Gen	$
Scruffy	2001-1	1992	3	45
Scruffy	5012	1991	2	70
Scruffy	5013	1992, 1995	3, 2	40, 75
Scrumptious	50022	9/29/06	4	10
Serena	80108	12/30/04	4	14
Serengeti	7425	2000	4	22
Shadow	1112	1998	1	250
Shadow	1129	2000	4	12
Shadow	5011	1994	2, 3	60, 45
Shaggington	5117	7/3/01	4	20
Shaggy	5303	1993	2	85
Shaggy	5304	1992	2	75
Shaggy	5305	1993	2, 3	75, 25
Shantou	20009	12/30/04	4	12
Sheriff	2039	1/1/01	4	15
Sherlock	1110	1990	1, 2	250, 125
Sherlock	2029	1988	3	25
Shivers	7419	1993	2	150
Shredder	20044	12/29/06	4	10
Silky	1004	1996	3	35
Skeeter	2039	9/29/06	4	12
Skimmer	7402	12/27/02	4	16
Skippy	2046	3/6/02	4	12
Skootch	5037	8/31/00	4	14
Slush	2045	12/28/01	4	10
Smokey	10017	4//28/06	4	18
Smokey	1005	1988	1, 2	1200, 100
Smokey	1005H	1988	1	1,200
Smokey	1005H	1986	1, 2, 3	1200, 300, 125
Smokey	1130	2000	4	15
Smokey	8016	1996	3	45
Sniffles	2021	1996	3	45

Skeeter

Skootch

Name	Style	Intro	Gen	$
Sniffy	2043	7/3/01	4	25
Snow Angel	56000	8/10/04	4	30
Snowball	2001	1986	1	1,000
Snowball	5002	1989	1	250
Snowball	5002	1991	2	150
Snowball	5002	1990	1	250
Snowfort	50014	1/31/06	4	11
Socks	1116	1993	2	200
Sofi	27001	10/18/05	4	10
Sophisticat	10021	12/29/06	4	20
Spanky	2010	1992	2	75
Spanky	2015	1996	3	20
Sparkles	8100	1997, 1999	3, 3	40, 35
Sparky	2004	1990	1, 2	275, 70
Sparky	2012	1994	3	45

Name	Style	Intro	Gen	$
Spice	1121	1998	3	30
Spice	5020	1996	3	40
Spout	7426	1996, 1998	3, 3	20, 20
Squirt	20007	1/31/05	4	12
Stardust	5627	11/1/03	4	30
Streaks	7439	6/30/05	4	16
Stretch	1131	2000	4	15
Stubbs	20032	6/30/06	4	12
Sugar	1138	4/30/02	4	20
Sugar	1138	12/1/01	4	20
Sugar	5007	1995	3	35
Sugar	5008	1990	1	175
Sugarbeary	57000	10/20/06	4	14
Sugarcane	53002	12/30/04	4	11
Sugarcoat	50016	6/30/06	4	10
Sugarplum	5042	1/1/01	4	20
Sunny	2028	1998	3	30
Sunset	50001	6/30/04	4	12
Super Arnold	9003	1990	1	350
Super Buddy	9006	1990	1	350
Super Chi-Chi	9004	1989	1	400
Super Fritz	9002	1989	1	350
Super George	9007	1990	1	350
Super Jake	7002	1988	1	250
Super Jake	9001	1989	1	400
Super Max	3002	1988	1	300
Super Max	3002	1990	2	250
Super Max	9001	1991	2	250
Super McGee	9005	1991	2	200
Super Petunia	9003	1989	1	350
Super Ping Pong	9010	1991	2	175
Super PJ	9010	1991	2	100

Stubbs

Sweeten

Name	Style	Intro	Gen	$
Super Schnapps	3002	1986	1	2,500
Super Scruffy	9000	1991	2	300
Super Scruffy	9011	1991	2	300
Super Snowball	9009	1991	2	300
Super Sparky	9002	1990	1, 2	300, 150
Super Tygger	9004	1990	1	400
Superdog	2058	2/28/03	4	15
Supersonic	70000	6/30/04	4	50
Sweeten	50024	11/30/06	4	10
Taffy	2014	1998	3	30
Taffy	2014	1996	3	20
Taffybeary	5315	2000	3	25
Tandy	20045	1/31/07	4	12
Tango (brown)	7000	1995	3	25
Tango (white)	7002	1995	3	25
Tangy	10026	1/31/07	4	12

Name	Style	Intro	Gen	$
Tanner	2054	10/31/02	4	14
Tapioca	50025	11/30/06	4	10
Tart	10025	1/31/07	4	12
Teddybearsary	5050	6/28/02	4	16
Teensy	7437	6/29/02	4	20
Thatcher	80119	1/1/06	4	14
Theodore	5501	1996	3	40
Thimbles	8038	12/27/02	4	15
Thomas	1139	12/28/01	4	20
Thunder	20040	10/31/06	4	15
Tidbit	2044	12/28/01	4	18
Timber	2002	1994	2, 3	100, 50
Tippi	20038	12/29/06	4	12
Toasty	50007	9/30/05	4	12
Toffee	2013	1993	2, 3	50, 35
Toffee	2032	2000	4	20
Topanga	70002	6/30/04	4	12
Tornado	7405	12/27/02	4	12
Trails	80128	4/30/07	4	12
Truly Yours	5134	12/31/03	4	25
Tucker	2065	12/31/03	4	30
Tugger	20008	12/30/04	4	12
Tugs	2062	6/30/05	4	12
Tulip	8008	1996	3	45
Tumbles	1008	1996	3	50
Twiddle	70020	12/29/06	4	12
Twiggy	7422	1991	2, 3	75, 45
Twitcher	8036	12/28/01	4	18
Tygger	1120	1990	1, 2	150, 60
Tygger	7420	1991	2	55
Tygger	7420	1994	2, 3	40, 30
Tygger	7420	1992	2	45

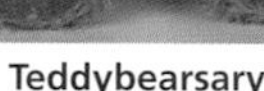

Teddybearsary

Woodside

Name	Style	Intro	Gen	$
Tygger	7421	1991	2	50
Tyler	27000	10/20/05	4	15
Vanilla	5012	1996	3	35
Wally	7423	1992	2	100
Wally	7423-1	1996	3	25
Walnut	5124	12/27/02	4	12
Weensy	7446	12/31/03	4	50
Wentworth	50011	1/1/06	4	11
Whinnie	8006	6/16/05	2, 3	55, 35
Whistles	50006	6/30/05	4	11
Willow	20021	1/1/06	4	12
Winston	2007	1991	2, 3	100, 40
Winthrop	5047	12/28/01	4	18
Woodside	50041	10/31/07	4	12

Yesterbear Brown

Yodeler

Name	Style	Intro	Gen	$
Woolly	8005	1996	3	22
Wuzzy	5202	1996	3	40
Wynter	2064	9/30/03	4	15
Xio Lin	5316	2/26/04	4	15
Yappy	2016	1998	3	20
Yappy	2016	1996	3	20
Yesterbear Brown	5028	2000	4	20
Yesterbear Cream	5029	2000	4	20
Yesterbear Yellow	5030	2000	4	20
Yodel	20035	8/31/06	4	35
Yodeler	20033	8/31/06	4	15
Yodels	20034	8/31/06	4	25
Yorkie	2006	1991	2, 3	75, 40
Yukon	7424	1996	3	50
Zephyr	70024	6/29/07	4	15
Zulu	7421	1994	2	175

Top Row: Elf, The Count, Santa
Bottom Row: Witch

Ty Gear

The Ty gear collection was introduced soon after the Beanie Kids launch in 2000. It includes kid clothing for the dolls, plus fun character costumes. It also includes three totes for carrying the dolls and their clothing—or anything else.

Baseball

Elf

Name	Style	Bday	$
Ballerina	508	9/22/00	5
Baseball	511	9/22/00	4
Beach Boy	515	7/31/01	4
Beach Girl	516	7/31/01	5
Bride	518	7/31/01	5
Bunny	512	1/1/01	9
Cheerleader	500	9/22/00	4
Doctor	509	9/22/00	4
Elf	525	11/1/01	4
Firefighter	506	9/22/00	4
Groom	519	7/3/01	6
In-Line Skater	517	7/3/01	4
Pajamas	503	9/22/00	8
Party Tyme	510	9/22/00	5
Princess	501	9/22/00	4

Princess

Summer Fun

Name	Style	Bday	$
Purple Leopard Ty Tote	601	2/28/03	8
Santa	523	11/1/01	5
School Days	505	9/22/00	5
Skeleton	522	9/3/01	6
Snowboarder	514	1/1/01	8
Soccer	502	9/22/00	5
Stars and Stripes	527	5/31/02	5
Summer Fun	504	9/22/00	4
Sunday Best/Dress Up	513	1/1/01	6
The Count	521	9/3/01	4
Ty-Dye Ty Tote	602	2/28/03	10
Uncle Sam	526	5/31/02	4
Witch	507	9/22/00	4
Yellow Flower Ty Tote	600	2/28/03	10

Jammin' Jenna, Rockin' Ruby, Sassy Star

Ty Girlz

In 2007 Ty introduced a collection of high fashion dolls for the "tween" and teen markets. The bodies are plush and feature rooted hair that can be styled, ranging in natural and fantasy colors. They have their own Web site entered by using the secret code on each hang tag. Girls can register for entertaining visits online. They can chat on a secure moderated web page, play games, decorate virtual houses, earn Ty money, go to the bank, shop at the mall, get makeovers, and try on clothes. All Girlz have 1st Generation hang tags.

Dazzlin' Destiny

Lovely Lola

Name	Style	Intro	Gen	$	Note
Bubbly Britney	2214	10/31/07	1	12	
Classy Carla	2210	7/12/07	1	12	
Cool Preppy	5205	3/2/08	1	5	outfit
Cute Candy	2208	7/12/07	1	12	
Cutie Cathy	2215	2/12/08	1	12	
Dazzlin' Destiny	2205	3/23/07	1	12	
Fairy Princess	5202	3/2/08	1	5	outfit
Girlz Night Out	5204	3/2/08	1	5	outfit
Happy Hillary	2216	2/12/08	1	12	
Jammin' Jenna	2209	7/12/07	1	12	
Lovely Lola	2204	3/23/07	1	12	
Lucky Lindsay	2212	10/3/07	1	12	
Precious Paris	2217	2/12/08	1	12	

Punky Penny

Sizzlin' Sue

Name	Style	Intro	Gen	$	Note
Pretty Patti	2207	7/12/07	1	12	
Punky Penny	2202	3/23/07	1	12	
Rockin' Ruby	2206	3/23/07	1	12, 15	blonde, brunette
Sassy Star	2203	3/23/07	1	12, 15	blue, pink lips
Sizzlin Sue	2201	3/23/07	1	12, 15	multi-colored hair, pink hair
Supercool Serena	2211	10/13/07	1	12	
Super Sporty	5201	3/2/08	1	5	outfit
Sweet Sammi	2218	2/12/08	1	12	
Totally Trish	2213	10/13/07	1	12	
Uptown Girl	5203	3/2/08	1	5	outfit

Top Row: Pocus, Ghoulianne, Hocus
Bottom Row: Creeps, Treats

Ty Halloweenies

The 3-inch Halloweenies are another holiday collection released in August for the Halloween season. They are much smaller than Beanie Babies and have ribbon loops sewn to their tops so they can be hung as decorations. Some Beanies are smaller versions of the regular sized ones. The smaller tags say Halloweenies on the front. All Halloweenies have 1st Generation hang tags.

BAT-e

Ghoul

Name	Style	Intro	$
BAT-e	35042	8/30/04	4
Creeps	35080	8/31/06	4
Fraidy	35043	8/30/04	4
Frights	35089	8/31/07	4
Ghosters	35058	8/31/05	4
Ghoul	35076	8/31/06	5
Ghoulianne	35077	8/31/06	4
Haunted	35092	8/31/07	4
Hocus	35055	8/31/05	4
Merlin	35057	8/31/05	4
Phantom	35091	8/31/07	4
Pocus	35056	8/31/05	5
Quivers	35041	8/30/04	5
SCARED-e	35044	8/30/04	5
Scarem	35093	8/31/07	4
Scream	35090	8/31/07	4
Screams	35079	8/31/06	4
Treats	35078	8/31/06	4
Tricky	35045	8/30/04	4

Haunted

Merlin

Screams

Tricky

Top Row: Snowgirl, Mistletoe, Santa
MIddle Row: Loosy, '97 Holiday Teddy, '99 Holiday Teddy, Quackers
Bottom Row: Twigs, Halo II, Rover

Ty Jingle Beanies

Jingle Beanies were first released in the fall of 2001 for the Christmas season. The 3-inch holiday Beanies feature ribbon loops for hanging, and many of them are a smaller version of a regular Beanie Baby. The first set did not include bells, but subsequent sets have a bell in each one. Only the four Decade Bears have bells on the outside. Some characters have variations. The smaller tags say "Jingle Beanies" on the front. All Jingle Beanies have 1st Generation hang tags.

2003 Holiday Teddy

Clubby II

Name	Style	Intro	$	Note
1997 Holiday Teddy	3506	9/17/01	3	button or stitched nose
1998 Holiday Teddy	3507	9/17/01	3	button or stitched nose
1999 Holiday Teddy	3508	9/17/01	3	button or stitched nose
2000 Holiday Teddy	3535	9/30/03	3	
2001 Holiday Teddy	3522	9/30/02	3	
2002 Holiday Teddy	3534	9/30/03	3	green or red body
2003 Holiday Teddy	35049	9/30/04	3	
Chillin'	3528	9/30/03	3	
Chillsy	35099	9/28/07	3	
Clubbies	3599	9/24/01	10	BBOC: box of 4
Clubby I	3599	9/24/01	4, 3	BBOC: button, stitched nose
Clubby II	3599	9/24/01	4, 3	BBOC: button, stitched nose
Clubby III	3599	9/24/01	4, 3	BBOC: button, stitched nose
Clubby IV	3599	9/24/01	4, 3	BBOC: button, stitched nose
Coldy	35094	9/28/07	3	
Cornbread	37002	11/10/04	5	Cracker Barrel

Decade (red)

Dizzy

Name	Style	Intro	$	Note
Decade	3536	10/1/03	3	gold body
Decade	3536	10/1/03	3	green body
Decade	3536	10/1/03	3	red body
Decade	3536	10/1/03	3	white body
Decades	3536	10/1/03	10	Ty Store: set of 4
Dizzy	3516	9/30/02	3	
Flakes	35082	9/29/06	7	
Flakesy	35096	9/28/07	3	
Flaky	3532	9/30/03	3	
Freezings	35086	9/29/06	4	
Gift (Joy)	37005	10/26/05	4	Hallmark: green
Gift (Love)	37004	10/26/05	4	Hallmark: white
Gift (Peace)	37003	10/26/05	4	Hallmark: red
Gifts	35063	9/30/05	4	
Goody	35062	9/30/05	4, 3, 3	smile center, left, right
Halo	3504	9/17/01	3	stitched or button nose

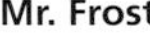

Mr. Frost

Gifts

Name	Style	Intro	$	Note
Halo II	3517	9/30/02	3	
Herald	3529	9/30/03	3	
Herschel	37001	11/10/04	5	Cracker Barrel
Icecaps	35085	9/29/06	4	
Icicles	35081	9/29/06	3	
Jangle	3531	9/30/03	3	
Jinglepup	3518	9/30/02	3	UK: green hat w/green tail
Jinglepup	3518	9/30/02	3	USA: green hat w/white tail
Jinglepup	3518	9/30/02	5	Singapore: white hat w/green tail
Jinglepup	3518	9/30/02	5	Canada: white hat w/white tail
Jingly	35097	9/30/07	3	
Kringles	35084	9/29/06	3	
Lil' Flakes	35703	10/31/07	4	Walgreen's
Lil' Freezes	35704	10/31/07	4	Walgreen's

Icicles

Patrick Claus

Name	Style	Intro	$	Note
Lil' Frosts	35705	10/31/07	4	Walgreen's
Lil' Sleds	35701	10/31/07	4	Walgreen's
Lil' Snow	35702	10/31/07	4	Walgreen's
Loosy	3501	9/17/01	3	
Melton	35050	9/30/04	3	
Mistletoe	3519	9/30/02	3	
Mr. Frost	35064	9/30/05	4	
Patrick Claus	35100	9/28/07	3	
Peace	3505	9/17/01	3	stitched or button nose
Presents	35065	9/30/05	4	
Quackers	3500	9/17/01	3	
Rover	3503	9/17/01	3	
Roxie	3530	9/30/03	3	
Rudy	35046	9/30/04	4	
Santa	3520	9/30/02	3	

Sleddy

Yummy

Name	Style	Intro	$	Note
Sleddy	35095	9/28/07	3	
Slushes	35083	9/29/06	3	
Snowgirl	3521	9/30/02	3	
SpongeBob JollyElf	35102	9/28/07	3	
SpongeBob SleighRide	35101	9/28/07	3	
Star	35048	9/30/04	3	
Sweetsy	35098	9/28/07	3	
The Beginning	3515	9/30/02	3	
Toboggan	35047	9/30/04	4	
Twigs	3502	9/17/01	3	
Twinkling	35066	9/30/05	3	
Yummy	35061	9/30/05	3	
Zero	3523	9/30/02	3	

Top Row: Quacks, Pinky
Bottom Row: Chocolate, Speedy, Patti

Ty® McDonald's Teenie Beanie Babies

Ty 1997 Teenie Beanie Babies

In 1997, Ty developed the ten 3-inch Teenie Beanie Babies exclusively for a McDonald's promotion. Although Ty made about ten million of each of its Teenie Beanie Baby characters and each was supposed to last a week, many McDonald's restaurants ran out of them within several days—and in some cases just hours. This promotion is now considered the most successful in fast-food history.

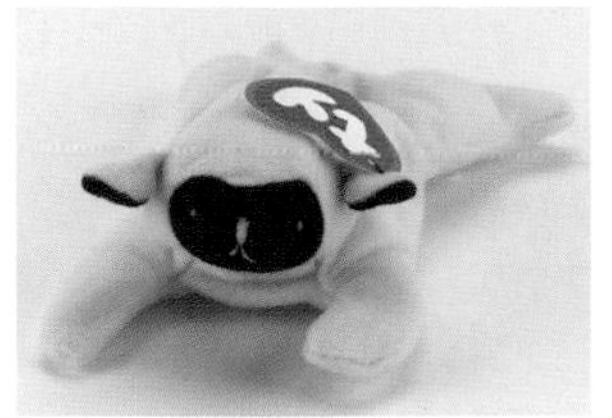

Chops

Speedy

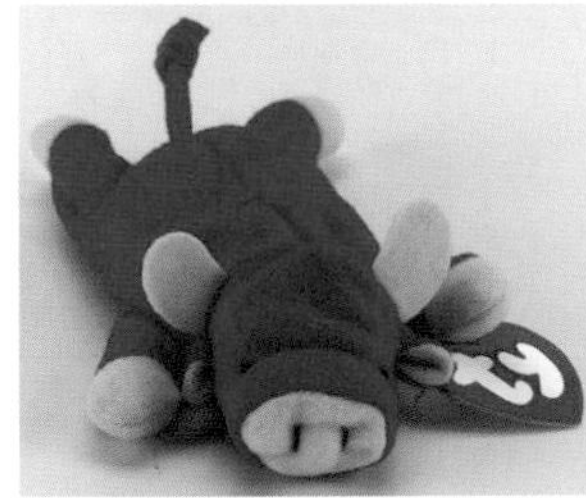

Snort

Quacks

Name	Style	Intro	Gen	$	Note
Chocolate	4	Apr-97	1	3	moose
Chops	3	Apr-97	1	3	lamb
Goldie	5	Apr-97	1	3	fish
Lizzy	10	Apr-97	1	3	lizard
Patti	1	Apr-97	1	3	platypus
Pinky	2	Apr-97	1	3	flamingo
Quacks	9	Apr-97	1	3	duck
Seamore	7	Apr-97	1	3	seal
Snort	8	Apr-97	1	3	bull
Speedy	6	Apr-97	1	3	turtle

Top Row: Inch, Waddles, Bongo, Twigs
Bottom Row: Peanut, Pinchers, Zip

Ty 1998 Teenie Beanie Babies

The 1997 Teenie Beanie Baby campaign was so popular that McDonald's repeated it the following year, this time offering twelve characters instead of ten and ordering approximately twenty million of each. The Teenie Beanie Baby craze further fueled the Beanie Baby mania, and prices began to skyrocket. Adults were no longer just giving them to their children as toys—they began collecting them as investments.

Happy

Scoop

Name	Style	Intro	Gen	$	Note
Bones	9	May-98	2	1	dog
Bongo	2	May-98	2	1	monkey
Doby	1	May-98	2	1	dog
Happy	6	May-98	2	1	hippo
Inch	4	May-98	2	1	worm
Mel	7	May-98	2	1	koala
Peanut	12	May-98	2	1	lt blue elephant
Pinchers	5	May-98	2	1	lobster
Scoop	8	May-98	2	1	pelican
Twigs	3	May-98	2	1	giraffe
Waddles	11	May-98	2	1	penguin
Zip	10	May-98	2	1	cat

Top Row: Strut, Erin, Maple, Britannia, Rocket
Bottom Row: Antsy, Smoochy, Freckles

Ty 1999 Teenie Beanie Babies

Once again, the overwhelming success of the previous year's Teenie Beanie Baby promotion prompted McDonald's to continue, this time increasing its line to sixteen characters, and for the first time, offering four international Teenie Beanie bears—Britannia (England), Erin (Ireland), Glory (United States), and Maple (Canada). A 1999 McDonald's Crew Bear was made just for their employees.

Chip

Iggy

Name	Style	Intro	Gen	$	Note
Antsy	2	May-99	3	1	anteater
Britannia	13	Jun-99	3	3	bear
Chip	12	May-99	3	1	cat
Claude	9	May-99	3	1	crab
Erin	14	Jun-99	3	3	bear
Freckles	1	May-99	3	1	leopard
Glory	15	Jun-99	3	3	bear
Iggy	6	May-99	3	1	iguana
Maple	16	Jun-99	3	3	bear
Nook	11	May-99	3	1	dog
Nuts	8	May-99	3	1	squirrel
Rocket	5	May-99	3	1	blue jay
Smoochy	3	May-99	3	1	frog
Spunky	4	May-99	3	1	dog
Stretchy	10	May-99	3	1	ostrich
Strut	7	May-99	3	1	rooster
Crew Glory	none	May-99	3	10	1999 McCrew Bear

Top Row: Spike, Bushy, Schweetheart, Springy
Bottom Row: Lips, Spinner, Tusk

Ty 2000 Teenie Beanie Babies

In the first 2000 campaign, the number of characters available was increased to eighteen. The fast-food chain also offered special issue Teenie Beanie Baby boxed sets during this promotion. A 2000 McDonald's Crew Bear was made just for their employees.

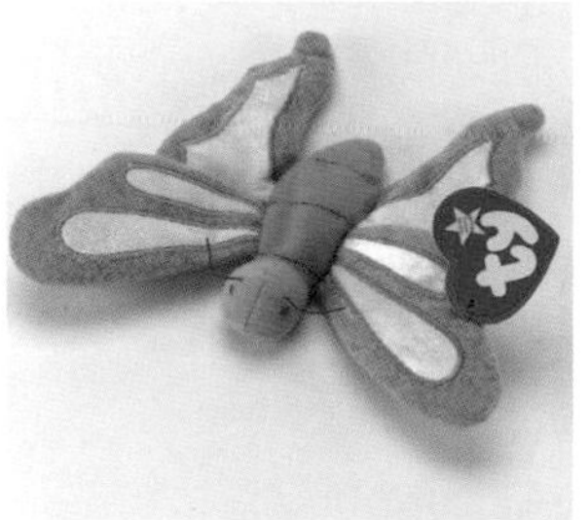

Flitter

Lucky

Name	Style	Intro	Gen	$	Note
Blizz	10	Jun-00	4	1	wt. tiger
Bumble	6	Jun-00	4	1	bee
Bushy	18	Jun-00	4	1	lion
Coral	14	Jun-00	4	1	fish
Dotty	4	Jun-00	4	1	dog
Flip	3	Jun-00	4	1	cat
Flitter	8	Jun-00	4	1	butterfly
Goochy	16	Jun-00	4	1	octopus
Lips	1	Jun-00	4	1	fish
Lucky	5	Jun-00	4	1	ladybug
Neon	13	Jun-00	4	1	seahorse
Schweetheart	12	Jun-00	4	1	orangutan
Slither	2	Jun-00	4	1	snake
Spike	11	Jun-00	4	1	rhino
Spinner	7	Jun-00	4	1	spider
Springy	17	Jun-00	4	1	bunny
Sting	15	Jun-00	4	1	manta ray
Tusk	9	Jun-00	4	1	walrus
Crew Millenium	none	Jun-00	4	10	2000 McCrew Bear

Top Row: Bronty, Millennium, Steg
Bottom Row: Osito, Peanut, Spangle

Ty 2000 Teenie Beanie Babies Boxed Sets

In the second 2000 Teenie Beanie Baby campaign, McDonald's offered several special collector's edition sets, with each character in its own plastic bubble-and-cardboard packaging. The sets available were a dinosaur trio, a U.S.A. trio, and international bear trio, a legends trio, a Ronald McDonald House Charities Millennium bear, and The End bear. A 2000 McDonald's Crew Bear was made just for their employees.

Humphrey

Libearty in package

Name	Style	Intro	Gen	$	Note
Bronty	20	Jun-00	4	3	dinosaur
Chilly	26	Jun-00	4	3	seal
Germania	23	Jun-00	4	3	bear
Humphrey	27	Jun-00	4	3	camel
Lefty	31	Oct-00	4	3	donkey
Libearty	29	Oct-00	4	3	bear
Millennium	32	Jun-00	4	3	bear
Osito	22	Jun-00	4	3	bear
Peanut	25	Jun-00	4	3	royal blue elephant
Rex	19	Jun-00	4	3	dinosaur
Righty	30	Oct-00	4	3	elephant
Spangle	24	Jun-00	4	3	bear
Steg	21	Jun-00	4	3	dinosaur
The End	28	Jun-00	4	3	bear

Top Row: Hamburglar, Birdie, Grimace
Bottom Row: Happy Meal, McNuggets, Burger, Golden Arches

Ty McDonald's Characters Teenie Beanie Babies

A final USA promotion in 2004 featured bears representing McDonald's characters. Overseas promotions were launched in 2005 and 2006 that included some of the same Teenie Beanies in the earlier collections. A 2004 Crew Bear was made just for McDonald's employees.

Fries

Ronald McDonald

Name	Style	Intro	Gen	$	Note
Big Red Shoe	10	Jul-04	6	2	bear
Birdie	3	Jul-04	6	2	bear
Burger	2	Jul-04	6	2	bear
Fries	11	Jul-04	6	2	bear
Golden Arches	4	Jul-04	6	2	bear
Grimace	12	Jul-04	6	2	bear
Hamburglar	9	Jul-04	6	2	bear
Happy Meal	7	Jul-04	6	2	bear
Happy Meal 25th Bear	1	Jul-04	6	3	bear
McNuggets	5	Jul-04	6	2	bear
Ronald McDonald	6	Jul-04	6	2	bear
Shake	8	Jul-04	6	2	bear

Ba Ba, Glide, Ribbit

Ty Pillow Pals

The first baby collection was introduced in 1995 and continued until the Baby Ty collection took its place. The first Pillow Pals were pale colors, but many of them were released later in bright color combinations. The eyes are embroidered for safety, and the later toys have larger eyes with a white highlight stitch in them.

Pillow Pals are simple in design, lay flat, and resemble the original Beanie Babies.

Name	Style	Intro	Gen	$	Note
Antlers	3028	1998	2	14	brown moose
Antlers	3104	1999	2	20	green moose
Ba Ba	3113	1999	2	14	purple lamb
Ba Ba	3008	1997	1, 1	20, 10	white lamb
Bruiser	3018	1997	1, 2	15, 10	tan bulldog
Carrots	3101	1999	2	11	green bunny
Carrots	3010	1997	1, 2	14, 12	peach bunny
Chewy	3105	1999	2	12	blue beaver
Clover	3020	1998	2	20	white bunny, black eyes
Clover	3020	1998	1, 2	17, 10	white bunny, blue/grey eyes
Foxy	3022	1998	1, 2	12, 11	tan fox
Glide	3025	1998	1, 2	12, 11	grey dolphin
Huggy	3002	1995, 1997	1, 1	14, 11	pink, blue ribbon
Huggy	3111	1999	2	12	yellow/red bear
Kolala	3108	1999	2	14	orange Koala
Meow	3011	1997	1	18	kittten
Meow	3107	1999	2	10	pink kitten
Meow	3011	1997	1, 2	11, 10	tan kitten
Moo	3004	1995	1, 2	14, 11	cream, b/w cow
Oink	3005	1995	1, 2	14, 11	pink pig
Paddles	3103	1999	2	12	green platypus
Paddles	3026	1998	2	11	fuchsia platypus
Purr	3016	1997	1, 2	15, 10	yellow/orange tiger
Red	3021	1998	1, 2	11, 10	red bull
Ribbit	3006	1995	1	30	green frog
Ribbit	3009	1997	1, 2	11, 10	green/yellow frog
Ribbit	3021	1998	2	12	red frog
Rusty	3100	1999	2	14	yellow raccoon
Sherbet	3112	1999	2	12	vivid ty-dye bear
Sherbet	3027	1998	2	12	pastel ty-dye bear

Snap

Zulu

Name	Style	Intro	Gen	$	Note
Snap	3015	1997	2	10	green/yellow turtle
Snap	3007	1995	1	45	yellow/brown turtle
Snap	3102	1999	2	12	ty-dye shell turtle
Snuggy	3001	1995, 1997	1, 1	20, 14	pink bear: pink, blue ribbon
Sparkler	3115	1999	2	10	red/white/blue bear
Speckles	3017	1997	1, 2	11, 10	spotted leopard
Spotty	3019	1998	1, 2	18, 10	b/w dog
Squirt	3013	1997	1	11	lt blue elephant: pink ears
Squirt	3109	1999	2, 2	14, 10	lt teal elephant: purple ears
Swinger	1998	1998	2	11	blue/yellow monkey
Swinger	3023	1998	1, 2	11, 10	brown monkey
Tide	3024	1998	1, 2	11, 10	b/w whale
Tubby	3012	1997	1, 2	15, 14	lavender hippo
Woof	3003	1995	1, 2	11, 10	cream, brown dog
Woof	3114	1999	2	10	orange/yellow dog
Zulu	3014	1997	1*, 1, 2	30*, 14, 11	*thick, thin stripes zebra

Top Row: Pinky Poo, Sugarcat, Bonita
Bottom Row: Baubles, Pupsicle

Ty Pinkys

Every Beanie in this collection introduced from 2004 through 2006 is pink. The animals range from 3" key-clips to the size of Buddies and Classics. Fabrics also vary from soft plush to curly fibers. Some characters come in several sizes and a few resemble Beanie Babies characters. There are also six purses and a Pinky's Pack that includes a tote filled with a Pinky Poo key-clip, a baseball cap, a T-shirt, and a lighted ballpoint pen. All Pinkys have 1st Generation hang tags.

Chenille

Dazzler

Name	Style	Intro	$	Note
Baubles	40205	6/6/04	7	
Bonita	40375	3/12/06	7	
Chenille	40210	11/4/04	7	
Chic	40213	2/28/05	7	
Dazzler	40203	4/9/04	7	
Dazzler Key-clip	40269	6/30/05	5	
Delights	44049	6/7/04	10	also red hang tag
Fab	40212	2/28/05	7	
Fanciful	40350	8/13/05	7	
Frilly	40204	5/2/04	7	
Frilly Key-clip	40399	none	5	
Gemma	40338	1/12/05	7	
Glitters	40207	10/15/04	7	
Glitters Key-clip	40333	12/30/05	5	

Gemma

Glitters

Name	Style	Intro	$	Note
Gloss	20013	2/28/05	12	
Hug Me	75005	1/31/06	7	
Julep	40206	7/11/04	7	
Julep Key-clip	40332	none	5	
Lil' Gloss	20014	2/28/05	10	
Love Me!	75007	1/31/06	7	
Minuet	40330	1/13/05	7	
Orchid	10007	2/28/05	12	
Paradise	20028	2/28/06	7	
Pinky Poo	40200	1/30/05	7	
Pinky Poo	none	none	50	NY Toy Fair: 5"
Pinky Poo	20011	2/28/05	12	large 12"
Pinky Poo Key-clip	40267	6/30/05	5	string legs
Pinky's Pack	44073	8/26/05	35	Ty Store: includes 5 items

Julep

Minuet

Name	Style	Intro	$	Note
Ballpoint Pen	44073	8/26/05		only w/Pinky's Pack
Baseball Hat	44066	8/26/05		only w/Pinky's Pack
Pinky Poo Key-clip	44063	8/26/05		only w/Pinky's Pack
Woman's T Shirt XL	44073	8/26/05		only w/Pinky's Pack
Woman's T Shirt L	44072	8/26/05		only w/Pinky's Pack
Woman's T Shirt M	44071	8/26/05		only w/Pinky's Pack
Woman's T Shirt S	44070	8/26/05		only w/Pinky's Pack
Girl's T Shirt 10-12	44068	8/26/05		only w/Pinky's Pack
Girl's T Shirt 6-8	44067	8/26/05		only w/Pinky's Pack
Poodle Caboodle	40363	3/31/06	12	dog purse
Pupsicle	44108	1/15/07	7	
Purrse	40337	1/31/06	12	cat purse
Radiance	40247	8/20/04	7	
Ratzo	40211	5/31/05	7	

Pinky Poo Key-clip

Pupsicle

Name	Style	Intro	$	Note
Ratzo	70007	12/28/05	15	large
Ratzo Key-clip	40268	6/30/05	5	
Rosa	40209	8/19/04	7	
Rosa Key-clip	40331	12/30/05	5	
Scribbly	20026	3/31/06	12	autograph dog
Shimmers	55003	2/28/05	12	
Silky	40201	2/21/04	7	
Silky the Key-clip	40398	6/30/06	5	
Smooches	40303	10/31/05	12	pink or red purse
Sparkles	40208	9/26/04	7	
Squeeze Me!	75006	1/31/06	7	
Style	40284	10/31/05	10	horse purse
Sugarcat	10014	1/31/06	12	
Taffeta	40202	3/14/04	7	
Twinkles	20012	2/28/05	10	

Ratzo

Rosa

Silky

Taffeta

Top Row: Slumbers, Puddles, Corkscrew, Winks
Bottom Row: Purrz, Plopper, Catnap

Ty Pluffies

Pluffies appeared in 2002 featuring a soft plush toy made from Tylux that is safe for babies. They are larger and more cushy than Beanie Babies and do not contain a rattle as do the earlier two baby lines, Pillow Pals and Baby Ty. Besides animals, they also include a pumpkin and several sports balls. Their sizes range from 5 inches to 12 inches. All Pluffies have 1st Generation hang tags.

Beary Merry

Bloose

Name	Style	Intro	$	Note
Baseball	32098	6/29/07	7	
Bashfully	32091	1/31/07	7	
Basketball	32070	2/28/06	7	
Beary Merry	32060	9/30/05	7	
Bloose	32077	6/30/06	7	
Bluebeary	3221	6/28/02	14	
Candy Cane	32061	9/30/05	7	
Castles	32093	4/30/07	7	
Catnap	3233	6/30/03	7	
Chills	37009	11/12/07	7	
Chomps	32066	1/31/06	7	
Clomps	32073	3/31/06	7	

Chomps

Cloud

Corkscrew

Dangles

Dotters

Name	Style	Intro	$	Note
Cloud	3223	6/28/02	18	
Corkscrew	3231	3/31/03	8	
Cruiser	3244	3/30/04	7	
Dangles	3226	3/31/03	7	
Dangles	32057	1/31/05	14	
Dotters	32074	6/30/06	7	
Ducky	32109	1/2/08	7	
Dreamsy	32107	11/30/07	7	
Flips	32097	6/29/07	7	
Football	32068	2/28/06	7	
Freeze	32102	9/28/07	7	
Freezer	32094	4/30/07	7	
Frost	32104	9/28/07	7	
Gallops	32065	1/31/06	7	

Gilly

Gobble

Harts

Kisser

Leapers

Name	Style	Intro	$	Note
Gilly	32087	12/29/06	7	
Gobble	32103	8/31/07	7	
Goodies	32050	9/30/04	7	
Googly	3238	12/30/03	7	
Gourdy	32059	8/31/05	7	
Grazer	3230	6/30/03	7	
Grins	3224	6/28/02	7	
Growlers	32067	1/31/06	7	
Harts	32085	11/30/06	9	
Icebox	32051	11/26/04	14	
Jingles	32082	9/29/06	8	
Kisser	32108	11/30/07	7	
Lasso	3246	3/30/04	8	
Leapers	32076	6/30/06	7	

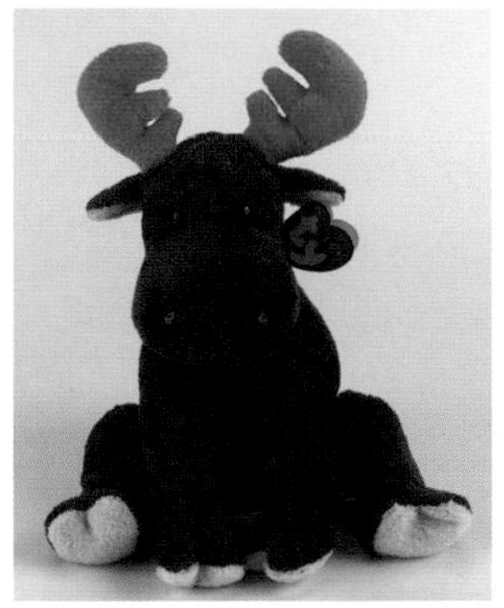

Lumpy

Melton

Name	Style	Intro	$	Note
Lil' Icebox	32052	11/26/04	9	
Lovesy	32053	11/30/04	13	
Lumpy	3235	9/30/03	9	
Melton	3236	9/30/03	10	
Merlin	32058	8/31/05	8	
Merry Moose	32083	9/29/06	8	
Milkers	32088	12/29/06	7	
Mr. Snow	32080	9/29/06	9	
Ms. Snow	32081	9/29/06	9	
Munches	32086	11/30/06	7	
Peppy	32099	6/29/07	7	
Piggy	32089	9/29/06	7	
Pinks	3220	6/28/02	12	
Plopper	3225	6/28/02	7	

Ms. Snow

Munches

Peppy

Pinks

Pookie

Puppers

Name	Style	Intro	$	Note
Plumpkin	32049	8/30/04	9	
Pokey	3241	12/30/03	8	
Ponds	32110	1/2/08	8	
Pookie	3243	3/30/04	10	
Pudder	3240	12/30/03	7	
Puddles	3222	6/28/02	7	
Puppers	3237	9/30/03	7	
Purrz	3234	6/30/03	7	
Quackies	32064	12/30/05	8	
Shearly	3245	3/30/04	12	
Shudder	32101	9/30/07	7	
Slumbers	3227	2/28/03	7	

Stomps

Twitches

Name	Style	Intro	$	Note
Snackers	32063	12/30/05	8	
Soccer Ball	32069	2/28/06	7	
Spooksie	32108	9/5/07	8	
Squeakies	32105	10/31/07	7	
Stomps	32071	3/31/06	7	
Sweetly	32084	11/30/06	8	
Tinker	3239	12/30/03	7	
Tiptop	32075	6/30/06	7	
Towers	32047	6/30/04	7	
Tromps	32072	3/31/06	8	
Tubby	3232	3/31/03	7	
Twitches	32090	1/31/07	7	

Waddles

Zips

Name	Style	Intro	$	Note
Twitchy	3242	1/30/04	10	
Waddles	32092	1/31/07	7	
Wades	32106	10/31/07	7	
Whiffer	3228	2/28/03	7	
Whiffer	32055	1/31/05	12	
Windchill	32048	9/30/04	9	
Wingers	37006	9/5/07	7	
Winks	3229	2/28/03	8	
Winks	32054	11/30/04	25	
Winks	32056	1/31/05	20	large
Wintery	37008	11/12/07	7	
Woods	32112	1/2/08	8	
Zips	32095	9/30/07	7	

Whiffer

Winks

Top Row: Treetop, Kitty, Zig-Zag, Pipsqueak
Bottom Row: Twizzles, Polka-Dot, Flipflop

Ty Punkies

The colorful and shaggy Punkies released in June 2002 feature another original fabric called TyTips®. It consists of soft stringy loops of thread, giving them a distinctive shaggy coat. Several of the Punkies come in several larger sizes. The entire collection of 51 is now retired. All Punkies have 1st Generation hang tags.

Butters

Flame

Name	Style	Intro	$	Note
Big Hugz	0435	11/30/04	50	extra-large
Big Kiss	0445	11/30/05	50	
Big Siren	0450	11/30/06	25	
Bitty Kiss	0444	11/30/05	12	
Butters	0422	12/30/03	8	
Dominoes	0418	9/30/03	8	
Flair	0431	10/29/04	7	
Flame	0420	11/26/03	8	
Flipflop	0409	12/27/02	7	
Frizzy	0400	6/28/02	10	
Great Big Hugz	0436	11/30/04	175	jumbo
Great Big Kiss	0446	11/30/06	175	jumbo
Hopscotch	0406	6/28/02	7	
Hugz	0437	1/20/05	20, 18	Buddy size: pink, white
Hugz	0434	11/30/04	7	white
Itty Bitty Kiss	0443	11/30/05	8	

Mambo

Marbles

Name	Style	Intro	$	Note
Jolly Santa Claws	0440	9/30/05	75	
Kitty	0415	4/30/03	10	
Lil' Hugz	0433	11/30/04	12	pink or white
Lil' Santa Claws	0442	9/30/05	7	
Lil' Siren	0447	11/30/06	8	
Mambo	0425	4/29/04	7	
Marbles	0423	12/30/03	7	
Pipsqueak	0411	12/27/02	10	
Polka-Dot	0408	12/27/02	7	
Polka-Dot	0429	10/29/04	15	large
Rainbow	0401	6/28/02	8	
Santa Claws	0441	9/30/05	12	
Screamers	0438	8/31/05	7	
Shockers	0424	12/30/03	7	
Shreds	0405	6/28/02	7	
Shriekers	0439	8/31/05	12	

Polka Dot

Rainbow

Shriekers

Shreds

Skitters

Splash

Name	Style	Intro	$	Note
Siren	0449	11/30/06	15	large
Sizzles	0407	11/27/02	10	
Skitters	0419	9/30/03	10	
Slim	0414	4/30/03	8	
Snort	0413	4/30/03	7	
Splash	0403	6/28/02	7	
Spookers	4401	9/27/04	12	Ty Store
Static	0416	9/30/03	7	
Swoosh	0427	4/29/04	7	
T-Bone	0410	12/27/02	10	
Topsy	0426	4/29/04	7	
Trapeze	0417	9/30/03	7	
Treetop	0412	4/30/03	7	
Tropics	0421	11/26/03	7	
Twizzles	0402	6/28/02	10	
Zapp	0428	4/29/04	10	
Zig-Zag	0404	6/28/02	7	
Zig-Zag	0430	10/29/04	12	large

Spookers

Static

Trapeze

Topsy

Top Row: Kool Katy, Playful Peggy, Home Run Hank, Rockin' Ruby, Jazzy Jessie, Footie,
Bottom Row: Witty Wendy, Midfield Mandy, Beautiful Belle, Chillin' Charlie, Dear Debbie

Ty Teenie Beanie Boppers

The 8-inch Teenie Beanie Boppers are a smaller version of the Beanie Boppers. Like their bigger version, they originally had their own page on the Ty website displaying information about their personalities and interests. They represent sports, professions, and interests of kids. Each doll has a loop on its back to hang or fasten to a backpack or purse. All Teenie Beanie Boppers have 1st Generation hang tags.

American Millie

Brave Buddy

Name	Style	Intro	$	Note
Ace Anthony	328	6/30/03	4	USA sports: tennis
American Millie	308	6/28/02	4	
BayStars Bruth	none	3/10/05	175	Yokohama BayStars
Beautiful Belle	313	9/30/02	4	
Blocka Bobby	110	9/25/03	8	Australia-New Zealand
Brave Buddy	320	9/30/02	5	
Captain	114	1/10/03	12	UK sports: soccer
Captain Colin	130	9/25/03	14	Australia-New Zealand
Caring Carla	326	1/30/03	5	
Change-Up Charlie	none	7/1/03	60	Ty MBNA: Cleveland Indians
Chillin' Charlie	324	1/30/03	4	
Classy Cassie	325	1/30/03	5	
Clean Up Clark	none	8/30/03	60	Ty MBNA: Chicago Cubs

Classy Cassie

Darling Daisy

Name	Style	Intro	$	Note
Cool Cassidy	304	6/28/02	5	
Crosscourt Cathy	327	6/30/03	5	
Cubby Casey	106	8/30/03	50	Wrigley Field, Chicago Cubs
Curve Ball Curt	none	8/1/03	60	Ty MBNA:Chicago White Sox
Darling Daisy	318	9/30/02	5	
Dear Debbie	312	9/30/02	5	
Disco Diva	336	4/29/04	5	
Footie	112	6/28/02	6	UK sports: soccer
Glitzy Gabby	306	6/28/02	5	
Hat Trick Hunter	111	6/28/02	5	Canada sports: hockey

Hat Trick Hunter

Paula Plappertasche

Name	Style	Intro	$	Note
Home Run Hank	319	9/30/02	5	USA sports: baseball
Hotshot	115	1/10/03	10	UK sports: soccer
Jazzy Jessie	302	6/28/02	4	
Kool Katy	317	9/30/02	5	
Lead Off Larry	none	7/31/03	60	Ty MBNA: Milwaukee Brewers
Lucky Linda	309	9/30/02	5	
Magic Molly	333	9/30/03	6	
Midfield Mandy	323	1/30/03	4	
Paula Plappertasche	113	6/28/02	6	
Playful Peggy	321	1/30/03	5	

Private Pete

Sassy Star

Name	Style	Intro	$	Note
Pretty Penelope	303	6/28/02	5	
Pretty Penny	311	9/30/02	5	
Private Pete	330	5/29/03	6	
Rockin' Ruby	310	9/30/02	5	
Rugged Rusty	300	6/28/02	5	
Sailor Sam	331	5/29/03	6	
Sassy Star	307	6/28/02	6	
Shy Shannon	316	9/30/02	6	
Sluggin' Steve	none	8/30/03	40	Ty MBNA: Seattle Mariners
Smashing Cherise	335	4/29/04	4	
Snappy Cindy	315	9/30/02	6	

Snazzy Sabrina

Sunny Sue

Name	Style	Intro	$	Note
Snazzy Sabrina	305	6/28/02	6	
Sunny Sue	314	9/30/02	5	
Suntory Sungoliath	132	10/15/04	10	Japan sports: rugby
Super Shuto	131	10/30/03	150	Japan sports: soccer
Sweet Sally	301	6/28/02	6	
Terrific Tessa	334	9/30/03	5	
Trendy Tracy	322	1/30/03	6	
Wahoo Wally	none	8/30/03	60	Jacob's Field, Cleveland Indians
Wishful Whitney	332	9/30/03	6	
Witty Wendy	329	6/30/03	5	

Kiss Me, You're a Cutie, Be Mine

Ty Valenteenies

The 3-inch Valenteenies are another holiday collection first released in November of 2005 for the Valentine Day's season. They are much smaller than Beanie Babies and have ribbon loops sewn to their tops so they can be hung as decorations. Each bear holds a satin heart. The smaller tags say "Valenteenies" on the front.

Name	Style	Intro	Gen	$
Be Mine Key-clip	35067	11/30/05	1	5
Kiss Me Key-clip	35068	11/30/05	1	5
You're a Cutie Key-clip	35069	11/30/05	1	5

1998 Winter Mass Collection:
Seal in Green Scarf, Polar Bear in Snowflake Hat, Walrus in Snowflake Cap, Penguin in Vest and Bowtie, Reindeer in Snowflake Scarf

Coca-Cola Bean Plush Toys

The Coca-Cola plush toy series by Cavanagh features several different collections made specifically for different markets. They include the International series, the Mass collection, and an upscale Beverly Hills collection. There are special sets for NASCAR, Sports, and Careers. They all include the recognizable bear and his friends in a variety of sizes and are often dressed in outfits. Many of them are holding a bottle of their favorite beverage in one hand.

Barris

Barrot

Coca-Cola International Series

The 1999 International series was released in five sets of ten, each representing a country where Coca-Cola is sold. Each plush toy's hang tag displays its national flag.

Clomp

Heeta

Name	Style	Animal	Country	$	Note
Ardie	248	aardvark	Niger	5	
Badgey	240	badger	Czech Repub	5	
Baltic	222	reindeer	Sweden	5	
Barris	235	brown bear	Russia	5	
Barrot	229	parrot	Brazil	5	
Blubby	250	pig	Vietnam	5	
Can Can	221	pelican	Cuba	5	
Clomp	217	elephant	Kenya	5	
Croon	225	baboon	Pakistan	5	
Crunch	245	crocodile	Sudan	5	
Curry	216	Bengal tiger	India	5	
Dover	213	bulldog	Great Britain	5	
Fannie	230	fox	Japan	5	
Gourmand	233	moose	Canada	5	
Heeta	249	cheetah	Namibia	5	

Lochs

Masa

Name	Style	Animal	Country	$	Note
Hopps	251	coki frog	Puerto Rico	5	
Howls	246	wolf	Romania	5	
Kelp	257	kiwi	New Zealand	5	
Key Key	237	snow monkey	Japan	5	
Laffs	243	llama	Bolivia	5	
Lochs	253	rabbit	Scotland	5	
Lors	234	wild boar	Italy	5	
Masa	220	lion	Mozambique	5	
Masha	260	ostrich	South Africa	5	
Meeska	255	hippo	Zambia	5	
Nardie	256	St. Bernard	Switzerland	5	
Neppy	254	proboscis monkey	Thailand	5	
Oppy	258	octopus	Greece	5	
Orany	247	orangutan	Singapore	5	
Paco	223	iguana	Mexico	5	

Ramel

Reegle

Name	Style	Animal	Country	$	Note
Peng	252	penguin	Chili	5	
Pock	238	peacock	Sri Lanka	5	
Quala	320	koala	Australia	5	
Ramel	238	camel	Egypt	5	
Reegle	311	eagle	USA	5	
Rhiny	232	black rhino	Tanzania	5	
Rifraff	224	giraffe	Somalia	5	
Rilly	218	gorilla	Rwanda	5	
Salty	226	sea turtle	Bahamas	5	
Streak	259	jackal	Tunisia	5	
Strudel	214	poodle	France	5	
Taps	231	tapir	Venezuela	5	
Toolu	212	toucan	Honduras	5	
Topus	241	zebra	Nigeria	5	
Toro	215	bulldog	Spain	5	

Waks

Woolsy

Name	Style	Animal	Country	$	Note
Vaca	227	longhorn cow	Argentina	5	
Waks	236	yak	Nepal	5	
Waller	242	walrus	Greenland	5	
Woolsy	244	sheep	Ireland	5	
Zongshi	228	panda	China	5	
Rare Exclusive					
Totonca	268	buffalo	USA	50	C C Collectors Society
2000 INTERNATIONAL					
Crooner	365	raccoon	USA	10	
Fire	343	flying dragon	Indonesia	10	
Duckles	333	Mandarin duck	Taiwan	10	
Jose	351	jaguar	Peru	10	
Tides	345	killer whale	Norway	10	
Sailor	330	swan	Austria	10	

Jeff Burton

Dale Earnhardt

Coca-Cola NASCAR Series

The NASCAR series features bears wearing a shirt or jacket with the number and signature of a NASCAR legend.

Name	$
Jeff Burton	5
Dale Earnhardt	5
Dale Earnhardt	5
D. Earnhardt Jr.	5
D. Earnhardt Jr.	5
Bill Elliot	5
Kenny Irwin	5
Dale Jarrett	5
Bobby Labonte	5
Steve Park	5
Adam Petty	5
Kyle Petty	5
Ricky Rudd	5
Tony Stewart	5

Dale Earnhardt

D. Earnhardt Jr.

D. Earnhardt Jr.

Bill Elliot

Kenny Irwin

Dale Jarrett

Bobby Labonte

Steve Park

Adam Petty

Kyle Petty

Ricky Rudd

Tony Stewart

Penguin in Chef's Hat

Polar Bear in Argyle Shirt

Coca-Cola Mass Collection

This collection features the bear and his friends dressed in Coca-Cola garb and holding a bottle of the beverage. They were sold in national regional and chain stores as well as gift and variety outlets. They appeared in sets in the spring and winter.

Husky with Coca-Cola Bottle

Whale with Coca-Cola Bottle

Name	Style	$	Note
MASS/HERITAGE SERIES			
Seal in Baseball Cap	0107	5	1997 Spring
Penguin in Delivery Cap	0108	5	1997 Spring
Polar Bear with Bottle	0109	5	1997 Spring
Polar Bear in Pink Bow	0110	5	1997 Spring
Polar Bear in Baseball Cap	0111	5	1997 Spring
Polar Bear in T-shirt	0112	5	1997 Spring
Seal in Scarf (red striped)	0101	5	1997 Winter
Seal in Snowflake Cap	0102	5	1997 Winter
Penguin in Stocking Cap	0103	5	1997 Winter
Polar Bear in Snowflake Cap	0104	5	1997 Winter
Polar Bear in Plaid Ribbon	0105	5	1997 Winter
Polar Bear in Red Bow	0106	5	1997 Winter
Penguin in Chef's Hat	0127	5	1998 Spring
Polar Bear in Argyle Shirt	0131	5	1998 Spring

Reindeer in Vest & Hat

Polar Bear in Soda Fountain Outfit

Polar Bear in Plaid Scarf

Penguin in Green Vest

Polar Bear in 2000 Top Hat

Polar Bear in 2000 Vest

Coca-Cola 2000 Millennium Collection

All members of this set have a special double tag in red "Exclusive" 2000 design. Each wears special apparel to mark the entry into the new century.

Seal in 2000 Vest

Penguin in 2000 Scarf

Name	Style	$	Note
Polar Bear in a 2000 Top Hat (boy)	0277	5	2000 Millennium
Polar Bear in a 2000 Vest (girl)	0278	5	2000 Millennium
Seal in a 2000 Vest	0279	5	2000 Millennium
Penguin in a 2000 Scarf	0280	5	2000 Millennium

Skier

Football player

Coca-Cola Sports & Career Series

Popular plush characters are dressed in sport uniforms or in clothing that represents different careers.

Name	Style	$	Note
Baseball player	0261	5	1999 Sport
Skier	0265	5	1999 Sport
Football player	0266	5	1999 Sport
Fireman	0310	5	2000 Career
Hockey player	0268	5	1999 Sport
Policeman	0312	5	2000 Career
Pilot	0315	5	2000 Career

Hockey player

Baseball player

Policeman

Pilot

Kickstart, Tanker, Clutch Carbo

Harley-Davidson Bean Plush Toys

This collection manufactured by Cavanagh includes a variety of characters, including bears, bulldogs, and pigs. Each is dressed with riding attire and accessories like jackets, helmets, boots, bandannas, or goggles.

Name	Animal	Intro	$
Big Twin	bear	1997	15
Boot Hill Bob	hog	1999	10
Bravo	bear	1999	10
Bubba	raccoon	1999	15
Clutch Carbo	hog	1998	9
Fat Bob	hog	1998	9
Kickstart	bear	1998	9
Manifold Max	bear	1998	9
Motorhead	bear	1997	12
Punky	hog	1997	12
Ratchet	hog	1997	12
Revit	Frog	1997	10
Roamer	bear	1997	12
Spotts	cow	1999	9

Big Twin

Boot Hill Bob

Bravo

Bubba

Name	Animal	Intro	$
Starke	skunk	1999	18
Stroker	black sheep	1999	19
Tanker	bulldog	1999	10
Thunder	bulldog	1999	15
Torque	bull	1999	20
Tusk	walrus	1999	12

Clutch Carbo

Fat Bob

Kickstart

Manifold Max

Motorhead

Punky

Ratchet

Revit

Roamer

Spotts

Starke

Stroker

Tanker

Thunder

Torque

Tusk

Glossary

1G, 2G, #G: 1st generation, 2nd generation, etc.

Authentic: A claim that a plush toy is a genuine manufactured product and not a fake. This does not mean it has been authenticated.

Authenticated: A claim by a reputable authentication service that it has verified that a product is genuine and not fake. These plush toys should be sealed in a clear box along with a certificate of authenticity.

Current: A plush toy still being produced and available for sale from the manufacturer and/or authorized dealers. It is not yet retired.

Discontinued: A plush toy no longer being manufactured but is not yet officially retired.

Exclusive: A plush toy distributed only for a particular country or event.

Fastener: The red (or older clear) piece of plastic that connects a hang tag to the plush toy.

Generation: The style of hang tag or tush tag attached to a plush toy. Tag generations are numbered in succession—1st generation, 2nd generation, etc.

Hang Tag: The cardboard tag attached to a plush toy. It is sometimes called a swing tag because it swings loosely from its fastener.

Heart Tag: (Also called a hang tag or swing tag) The tag is shaped like a heart, usually located near the top of the plush toy, such as on an ear. This tag usually includes a logo and important information.

Internet Exclusive: A Ty product that can only be ordered online through the Ty Store section of the Ty Web site.

Locket: Some tag protectors or hang tags that open like a hinged locket.

Loved: Usually means a plush toy has been played with and loved by a child. Usually not in mint condition—missing tags, damaged tags, worn look to the fur, etc.

Mint: Term referring to a plush toy or tag in perfect, new condition.

Pooh Face: The nickname given to the newest faced Ty bears created since 2000. They have a "Pooh" appearance to them, including large bellies.

Retired: A plush toy that has been officially declared out of production. Typically only available on the secondary market.

Secondary Market: Merchandise is offered to the consumer by means other than a retail or wholesale channel. Usually found on auction sites.

Secondary Market Value: The amount an item is worth in the secondary market.

Sports Promotion: A plush toy that has been given away at a sporting event. They typically come with a card.

Swing Tag (also called heart or hang tag): The heart-shaped tag usually located near the top of the plush toy, such as on an ear. This tag usually includes a logo and important information.

Tag Protector: A clear plastic cover that slides or folds over a hang tag to keep it protected.

Tush Tag: The cloth tag containing manufacturing information that is sewn into the seam of a plush toy, usually on its bottom.

Ty: Ty or Ty Inc. is the name of the company that produces Ty Beanie Babies. The name is derived from H. Ty Warner, the name of the founder of the company and creator of Beanie Babies.

Tylon: A soft fabric used exclusively for Beanie Babies.

Tyhair (Tysilk): A fabric used in several products distributed by Ty. This fabric is used mostly on Beanie Babies.

Variation: A plush toy that a manufacturer has intentionally changed. Manufacturers most commonly modify a plush toy's color.

Online Auction Acronyms

Following are the most common abbreviations used in online auction descriptions.

BIN: *Buy it now.*

BBOT: Beanie Baby Board of Trade. A feature on the Ty.com Web site where people can place ads to buy, sell, or trade Ty products.

BBOM: Beanie Baby of the Month. A Ty club that sent a new Beanie Baby to members each month. Discontinued the end of 2007.

BBOC: Beanie Baby Official Club. The official Ty club.

CC: Credit card.

GC: Good condition.

GA: Guaranteed authentic.

EX: Excellent condition.

MIP: *Mint in package*. Usually refers to a plush toy in its original packaging.

MWBMT: *Mint with both mint tags.* Means both hang tag and tush tag are in mint condition.

MMBT: *Mint with bent tag.*

MWCHT: *Mint with creased hang tag.*

MWHT: *Mint with hang tag.*

MWMT: *Mint With mint tags*. Means both hang tag and tush tag are in mint condition.

MWNT: *Mint with no tags.*

MWNMT: *Mint with non-mint tags*. Means the plush toy itself is in mint condition, but its tags are not. This can mean it doesn't have a tag or the tag is not in mint condition.

MWT: *Mint with tag.*

NF: This refers to the "new face" on Ty Beanie Baby bears when they have a stitch across the nose. Nearly all releases since 1997 have had this new face.

NM: *Near mint condition.*

NR: *No reserve.*

OF: The "old face" on Ty Beanie Baby bears without a stitch across the nose. The OF Teddies are generally more valuable, since they are an older style and hard to find.

PE: Polyethylene pellets, which are tiny plastic beans used to stuff early bean plush toys.

PLMK: *Please let me know*. Often used in trading and selling posts when a poster is waiting to hear from someone.

HTF: *Hard to find*. Usually refers to plush toys that are in high demand and difficult to find. Often they are retired.

ISO: *In search of*. Used on trading boards when people want to trade for a certain plush toy.

LE: *Limited Edition.* A plush toy manufactured in much lower quantities than other releases of its kind, increasing its value.
PP: PayPal, a service for making purchases.
PVC: Polyvinylchloride pellets, which are the older type of pellets used to fill bean plush toys. They are thought to be of higher quality than the newer PE pellets. PVC pellet-filled plush toys often sell for two to three times more on the secondary market.
S/H: Shipping and handling.
VG: *Very good condition.*
VHTF: *Very hard to find.* Usually used when referring to a rare plush toy.
WTT: *Willing to trade.*

Garfield Goodnight

Bean-Filled Ambassadors

Although bean plush toys are treasured by collectors, their greatest value may be in the joy they bring to children. If you have a valuable bean plush toy, display it proudly in your collection or sell it to another collector. But if you want to dispose of well-loved plush toys with torn or creased tags, consider donating them to a hospital, shelter, charity, or to children in Iraq or Afghanistan. The colorful squishy toys are especially wanted and needed in those countries, as they have had an astonishingly powerful impact in bridging cultural, political, and religious barriers, earning them the title of bean-filled ambassadors.

Read about their amazing work overseas and get information on how to donate them by visiting the following Web sites:

www.beaniesforbaghdad.com

www.operationiraqichildren.org

www.beyondorders.org/home.asp

www.spiritofamerica.net